# The Middle Eastern Kithchen

===========================================

A Complete Cookbook Inspired by Middle Eastern recipes

Qasim Labib

# INTRODUCTIONS

## WHAT IS RECIPE BOOK?

A recipe book is a collection of instructions or guidelines for preparing various dishes or meals. It typically includes recipes for appetizers, main courses, side dishes, desserts, and drinks, among others. A recipe book can be written by a professional chef, a cooking enthusiast, or anyone who wants to compile their favorite recipes in one place. The recipes in a recipe book usually include a list of ingredients needed, step-by-step instructions on how to prepare the dish, and sometimes tips and tricks for getting the best results. Recipe books can be in physical form, such as a printed book, or in digital form, such as an e-book or website.

## WHAT ARE THE MIDDLE EASTERN COUNTRIES?

The Middle East is a region located at the crossroads of Asia, Africa, and Europe. It is comprised of countries that are predominantly Muslim and Arab-speaking, although there are also other ethnic and linguistic groups present.

The countries in the Middle East include:

- Bahrain
- Cyprus
- Egypt
- Iran
- Iraq
- Israel
- Jordan
- Kuwait
- Lebanon
- Oman
- Palestine
- Qatar
- Saudi Arabia
- Syria
- Turkey
- United Arab Emirates
- Yemen

## HOW RECIPE BOOKS HELP TO COOK?

A recipe book is an essential tool that helps to cook by providing detailed instructions for preparing a wide variety of dishes. Here are some ways in which a recipe book can help you in your cooking:

- **Provides guidance:** A recipe book provides step-by-step instructions on how to prepare a dish. It tells you what ingredients you need, how much of each ingredient to use, and the order in which to combine them. This helps you to ensure that you are following the recipe correctly and that the dish turns out as intended.

- **Ensures consistency:** When you follow a recipe, you can be sure that the dish will turn out consistently every time. This is especially important if you are preparing a dish for a special occasion or for guests.
- **Offers new ideas:** A recipe book can inspire you to try new ingredients or cooking techniques that you may not have considered before. This can help you to expand your culinary skills and repertoire.
- **Saves time:** By using a recipe book, you can save time by not having to figure out the details of a dish on your own. This is especially useful when you are in a hurry or have limited time to prepare a meal.
- **Helps with planning:** A recipe book can help you plan your meals in advance by providing you with a range of ideas for breakfast, lunch, and dinner. This can help you to ensure that you are eating a balanced and varied diet.

# THE BOOK IS CONTAINING :

The book contains around **100** middle eastern food recipes . Including meals, snacks and dessert items.

## The book contains on an average -

- 40 meals recipes
- 35 snacks recipes
- 25 desert recipes

### With containing their-

- Preparation Time
- Cooking Time
- Resting Time &
- Servings

## CONCLUSION:

This book will help to understand and learning middle eastern recipes to the beginner and also provide a good impression on various delicious food items to the reader. It will also help to understand the various traditional culture of different countries.

- SPICY LENTIL SOUP — 88
- Fattah — 89
- Ful Buried — 91
- Homemade Egyptian Hawawshi — 92
- SLOW COOKER EGYPTIAN LENTILS AND RIC — 94
- EGYPTIAN TOMATO SAUCE — 95
- Sriracha Deviled Eggs with Spicy Bread Crumbs — 95
- chicken shawarma — 97
- Egyptian Mahlab bread — 98
- Salata Baladi — 99
- EGYPTIAN GARLIC YOGURT CUCUMBER SALAD — 100
- Toum Recipe for the World's Strongest Lebanese Garlic Sauce — 101
- BEST EVER OM ALI (EGYPTIAN BREAD PUDDING) — 102
- Melt-In-Mouth Butter Cookies (Egyptian Ghorayebah) — 103
- Majboos/ Kabsa – Meat And Vegetables Rice — 104
- Gursan – Meat And Vegetable Stew — 105
- Jalamah – Arabian Lamb Stew — 106
- Dajaj Mashwi – Arabian Grilled Chicken — 107
- Ruz Al Bukhari – Fragrant Rice And Roasted Chicken — 108
- Tharid/ Thareed – Meat And Vegetable Stew Over Crispy Bread — 110
- Jareeshs – Crushed Wheat With Meat — 111
- Saleeg – Roasted Meat & Creamy Rice — 113
- Mandi – Chicken Rice — 115
- Masoub ~ Saudi Banana Bread Mash — 118
- SOBIA DRINK — 119
- JALLAB — 120

| | |
|---|---|
| Jordanian Mansaf | 120 |
| Labneh (Strained Yogurt) | 122 |
| Manaqish \| Jordanian Zaatar Flatbread ~ J for Jordan | 122 |
| Kousa Mahshi (Stuffed Zucchini) | 123 |
| Warak Enab- Stuffed Grape Leaves | 125 |
| Kibbeh | 127 |
| Musakhan (Palestinian Roast Chicken with Sumac and Flat Bread) | 128 |
| JORDANIAN MANSAF | 130 |
| Sayadieh | 131 |
| Egg Salad | 133 |
| Chicken Shawarma Rice | 133 |
| Freekeh | 135 |
| **THE END** | **136** |

# RECIPE STARTS

## POMEGRANATE CHICKEN WITH ALMOND COUSCOUS

Prep Time: 5 minutes

Cook Time: 15 minutes

Servings: 4 servings

## INGREDIENTS

- 1 tbsp vegetable oil
- 200g couscous
- 1 chicken stock cube
- 1 large red onion, halved and thinly sliced
- 600g chicken mini fillets
- 4 tbsp tagine spice paste or 2 tbsp harissa
- 190ml bottle pomegranate juice (not sweetened; we used Pom Wonderful)
- 100g pack pomegranate seeds
- 100g pack toasted flaked almond
- small pack mint, chopped

## INSTRUCTIONS

**1.** Heat up the pot and intensity the oil in an enormous skillet. Season the couscous and crumble it into half of the stock cube in a bowl. Add the onion to the dish and sear for a couple of mins to relax. Cover the bowl with a tea towel and set aside after just covering the couscous with boiling water.

**2.** Add the chicken fillets and brown on all sides, pushing the onion to one side of the pan. After incorporating the pomegranate juice and tagine paste or harissa, crumble in the remaining stock cube and season to taste. Cover and simmer for 10 minutes, or until the chicken is cooked through and the sauce has thickened. Stir in the pomegranate seeds, keeping some for garnishing before serving.

**3.** Mix the almonds and mint into the couscous with a fork after 5 minutes. Place the chicken on top of the couscous and spoon over the sauce.

# LEBANESE MOUSSAKA (MAGHMOUR)

Prep Time: 10 minutes

Cook Time: 50 minutes

Servings: 4-6 servings

## INGREDIENTS

- 1 kg aubergine (eggplant)
- 130 ml olive oil (I use a mild extra virgin)
- 1 onion, finely chopped
- 5 garlic cloves, finely chopped
- 2 tsp ground allspice
- 1 tsp ground cinnamon
- 800 g tomatoes, skinned and chopped (fresh or tinned)
- 2 tsp sugar
- 1 Tsbp lemon juice
- 500 g cooked chickpeas (from 200 g dry chickpeas or 2x400 g tins)
- water
- finely chopped flat-leaf parsley, to garnish
- salt and pepper

## INSTRUCTIONS

1) The oven should be preheated to 230 C (445 F) fan. Use baking parchment to line two baking sheets.
2) Slice the aubergine into cubes measuring 12 cm (1 in) in diameter after peeling off the skin's stripes in a pattern resembling a zebra. Combine with some salt and 100 milliliters of olive oil. Roast for about 15 minutes on each of the two baking sheets, or until almost completely softened. I position the two baking sheets in the middle of the oven high. If one cooks faster than the other, keep an eye on them and switch places (this varies widely between ovens). Place aside.
3) Heat a pot with a thick bottom over medium-low heat. Sear the onion in the excess 2 Tbsp (30 ml) olive oil until relaxed, however not shaded, blending consistently. This generally requires 8-10 minutes. With a little bit of salt and pepper, add the cinnamon, allspice, and garlic. Add the tomatoes, sugar, and 100 milliliters of water after 30 seconds of constant stirring. Combine thoroughly, bring to a boil, and cover and simmer for 10 to 15 minutes to let the flavors settle.
4) Roasted aubergine, cooked chickpeas, and lemon juice should be added. Cover and cook for another 10 to 20 minutes, or until the aubergine is completely soft. Add more salt, pepper, sugar, or lemon juice to taste for seasoning.

5) Sprinkle generously with finely chopped flat-leaf parsley for a generous garnish when serving warm or at room temperature.

## MOUSSAKA

Prep Time: 7 minutes

Cook Time: 10 minutes

Servings: 4 servings

## INGREDIENTS

- 2 brown pittas, torn into pieces
- 5 tbsp olive oil
- 2 lemons, juiced
- 1 garlic clove, crushed
- 250g block halloumi, sliced
- 250g microwavable pouch quinoa
- 350g medium tomatoes, quartered
- 1 large cucumber, halved, deseeded and sliced
- 4 spring onions, sliced
- ½ small bunch mint, chopped
- ½ small bunch dill, roughly chopped

## INSTRUCTIONS

1. Turn up the heat on the grill. Spread the pitta pieces out on a baking sheet and toss them with one tablespoon of oil. Barbecue for 3-4 mins, turning most of the way, until brilliant and fresh. Reserve for cooling.
2. Season after combining the remaining oil, lemon juice, and garlic in a bowl. Cook the halloumi for 1-2 minutes on each side, or until lightly charred, in a large griddle pan or nonstick frying pan over high heat.
3. Toss the quinoa with the tomatoes, cucumber, spring onions, most of the fresh herbs, and the dressing after cooking it according to the package's instructions. Season as desired. Place the pita, halloumi, and remaining herbs on top of the dish and place it on a serving plate.

# MUSABAHA / MASABACHA (WARM CHICKPEAS IN TAHINI SAUCE)

Prep Time: 10 minutes

Cook Time: 65 minutes

Servings: 2-3 servings

## INGREDIENTS

- 500 g boiled chickpeas (from 200 g dried chickpeas (see below) or 2x400 g tinned, rinsed and drained)
- 125 ml chickpea cooking water or drinking water
- 50 g (3 Tbsp) tahini
- 1 tsp ground cumin
- 1 Tbsp lemon juice, or to taste
- salt and pepper

## CHICKPEAS:

- 200 g dried chickpeas
- 1 bay leaf
- 1 whole garlic, cut in half horizontally (no need to peel)
- water
- salt

## TOPPING:

- 3 Tbsp extra virgin olive oil
- 20 g pine nuts
- 3 garlic cloves, thinly sliced
- a generous handful of flat-leaf parsley (without thick stalks), finely chopped
- 1 tsp Aleppo pepper or to taste

## INSTRUCTIONS

1. Put at least three times as much water as the chickpeas. Sprinkle on a good amount of salt. Allow to soak for at least eight hours, or overnight, in a cool location. Place them in the refrigerator if you plan to leave them for more than 12 hours or if your kitchen is very warm.
2. Remove the chickpeas from the water. Add additional teaspoon salat and fresh water to cover by 2 to 3 cm. While skimming the foam from the surface, bring to a boil and boil vigorously for three to four minutes. Turn the intensity down to low, carrying the water to a sluggish stew with just slight development on a superficial level. Include the garlic, olive oil, and bay leaf. Pass on to stew like this until the chickpeas are totally delicate. It might take anything from 20 minutes to a few hours, contingent upon your chickpeas,

however they're typically finished in 30-45 minutes. Test frequently and keep an eye on it closely. Remove the chickpeas from the heat and discard the bay leaf and garlic when you are satisfied that they are done. Check at least three chickpeas before removing from the heat because the chickpeas may cook unevenly.

3. Add the chickpeas to a bowl while they are still warm, along with 125 milliliters of the cooking water, tahini, ground cumin, and lemon juice. Utilizing a fork, generally pound until the surface is as you would prefer. Salt, pepper, and additional lemon juice can be added to taste. Individual serving bowls or a large communal bowl can be used to serve the msabbaha.
4. In a small saucepan, heat pine nuts, 3 Tbsp extra virgin olive oil, and thinly sliced garlic cloves simultaneously over medium heat. Fry with constant stirring until golden but not burned. It ought to only take a few minutes. If you don't immediately add the garlic and pine nuts to top your msabbaha, they will continue to cook in the hot oil. As a result, you should do this at the very last minute.
5. The oil, pine nuts, and garlic topping should be added to the bowls of msabbaha. Flat-leaf parsley and chili flakes should be added on top. Serve right away.

## SUMMER COUSCOUS SALAD

Prep Time: 10 minutes

Cook Time: 40 minutes

Passive Time: 5 minutes

Servings: 4 servings

## INGREDIENTS

- 250g couscous
- 250ml vegetable stock, boiling
- 400g can chickpeas, drained and rinsed
- 1-2 tbsp vegetable or olive oil
- 300g courgette, sliced on the slant
- 300g small v ine-ripened tomatoes
- 250g pack halloumi cheese, thickly sliced and then halved lengthways, halved

**For the dressing:**

- 125ml olive oil
- 3 tbsp lime juice
- 2 large garlic cloves, finely chopped
- 2 tbsp chopped fresh mint
- ½ tsp sugar

## INSTRUCTIONS

1. Tip the couscous into a bowl, pour the bubbling stock over and blend well in with a fork. Leave for four minutes and cover with a plate. In the meantime, combine all of the dressing ingredients thoroughly in a bowl. Use a fork to fluff the couscous, then stir in the chickpeas and half the dressing. Add everything to a large serving dish and mix well.
2. In a large frying pan, heat 1 tablespoon of oil and fry the courgette slices for 2 to 3 minutes, or until they are a deep golden brown. Transfer to kitchen paper. Now, place the cut-side-down tomatoes in the pan and cook for a few more minutes until the underside is slightly browned. Place the courgettes and tomatoes on top of the couscous.
3. If the pan is dry, add a little more oil and heat it. Add the halloumi strips and fry them for 2 to 3 minutes, turning them over halfway through, until they are crispy and have a brown sizzle to them. Spread the remaining dressing over the top of the tomatoes. Serve as quickly as you can.

## SILKY SMOOTH AND CREAMY HUMMUS

Prep Time: 5 minutes

Cook Time: 15-35 minutes

Servings: A large or few small plates

## INGREDIENTS

- 100 g dry chickpeas
- 1 tsp bicarbonate of soda
- 100 g tahini
- juice of 1/2 lemon
- 2 cloves of garlic, peeled
- 1/4-1/2 tsp ground cumin (optional)
- 1/2 tsp salt
- cooking water from the chickpeas
- extra virgin olive oil, to serve
- cumin or paprika, to serve (optional)
- flat-leaf parsley, to serve (optional)

## INSTRUCTIONS

1. Absorb the chickpeas somewhere multiple times their volume water for no less than 4 hours, ideally short-term. Change the water, add the bicarbonate of pop and bring to the bubble. Bring down the intensity and pass on to stew until delicate, anything from 25 minutes to an hour or more - this can differ altogether from one clump to another. When you can easily mash the chickpeas by gently squeezing them between your fingers, they are done. Reserve the cooking water after draining it. Reserve some of the chickpeas with the most beautiful appearance for garnish.
2. In a food processor, combine the chickpeas, tahini, lemon juice, garlic, 100 milliliters of cooking water, cumin (if using), and salt while it is still warm. Process until completely smooth and a little fluffy, at least three to four minutes. Allow it to run for another minute or two after it appears finished.) Taste and adjust the flavors or seasonings to your liking. The hummus will be fairly runny at this point, but don't worry; once it cools, it will set. Cover with plastic wrap directly on top of the hummus after transferring to a bowl. Between the hummus and the plastic wrap, there should be no air. Allow to cool. Put it in the refrigerator to speed things up if you're short on time.
3. Serve on at least one plates little plates. Make the bowl's distinctive dimples with the back of a spoon. If you like, garnish with the reserved chickpeas, some spices, chopped flat-leaf parsley, and a generous drizzle of extra virgin olive oil.

## SHAKSHUKA

Prep Time: 5 minutes

Cook Time: 20 minutes

Servings: 2 servings

## INGREDIENTS

- 1 tbsp olive oil
- 2 red onions, chopped
- 1 red chili, deseeded and finely chopped
- 1 garlic clove, sliced
- small bunch coriander stalks and leaves chopped separately
- 2 cans cherry tomatoes
- 1 tsp caster sugar
- 4 eggs

## INSTRUCTIONS

1. In a frying pan with a lid, heat the oil and cook the onions, chili, garlic, and coriander stalks for five minutes until soft. Mix in the tomatoes and sugar, then, at that point, bubble for 8-10 mins until thick. able to be frozen for one month.

2. Make four dips in the sauce with a large spoon and crack an egg into each one. Put a top on the container, then cook over a low intensity for 6-8 mins, until the eggs are finished however you would prefer. Serve with crusty bread and scatter with the coriander leaves.

# FATTOUSH

Prep Time: 15 minutes

Cook Time: 20 minutes

Servings: 3-4 portions

## INGREDIENTS

- 1 pita, halved into two rounds, 1 large lavash or other bread, cut into triangles/pieces
- 2-3 tbsp olive oil
- 2 medium (c. 250 g) tomatoes, cut into chunks
- 3 small cucumbers (c. 250 g), cut into chunks
- 3-4 small radishes (c. 100 g), cut into chunks
- 3 spring onions, sliced thinly
- 12-15 stalks flat leaf parsley (c. 30 g), leaves only, roughly chopped
- 4-5 stalks mint (c. 12 g) mint, leaves only, finely sliced
- 2 tbsp lemon juice
- 4 tbsp extra virgin olive oil (I use a mild variety)
- 2 tsp sumac, plus extra to garnish
- salt

## INSTRUCTIONS

1. The oven should be preheated to 200 C fan.
2. With love oil, combine the pita or other bread. Distribute on a roasting tray, avoiding overlapping pieces. Cook until firm, however not consumed, 5-10 minutes, contingent upon the size and thickness of your bread pieces. To cool, transfer to a rack with wires. In place of roasting, you can fry the bread in a large frying pan, tossing frequently, for a few minutes until browned on the edges and beginning to turn crispy.
3. In a large bowl, toss the vegetables with a little salt. Put it aside for a few seconds.
4. Toss the vegetables well with the sumak, olive oil, herbs, and lemon juice. Toss once more after adding the toasted bread. Serve right away.

# TABBOULEH SALAD

Prep Time: 15-20 minutes

Servings: 4 servings

## INGREDIENTS

- 250g couscous
- 4 vine-ripened tomatoes
- half a cucumber
- 1 bunch spring onions, sliced
- 2 x 20g packs fresh parsley
- grated zest of a lemon
- 6 tbsp olive oil
- 2 tbsp lemon juice
- 1 crushed garlic clove

## INSTRUCTIONS

1. Get the couscous ready: Place the couscous in a substantial bowl. Stir after pouring over the boiling stock or water. Cover with a plate or cling film and let stand for five minutes until all the liquid is absorbed. Grease the grains with a fork to separate them.
2. Cucumber and vine-ripened tomatoes should be finely diced. The spring onions should be sliced and the parsley should be finely chopped before being added to the couscous along with the lemon zest.
3. Drizzle the olive oil, lemon juice, and garlic over the couscous after thoroughly seasoning it. Serve with some grilled fish, meat, or chicken and a thorough toss.

# BABA GANOUSH

Prep Time: 5 minutes

Cook Time: 10 minutes

Servings: 1 plate

## INGREDIENTS

- 2 large aubergines (c. 600-700 g total weight)
- 1 clove of garlic, crushed to a paste with a generous pinch of salt
- 2 tbsp lemon juice
- 2 tbsp tahini
- 2 tbsp extra virgin olive oil, to garnish
- 2 tbsp pomegranate seeds or 1 tbsp chopped fresh mint, to garnish
- salt

## INSTRUCTIONS

1. Prick the aubergines a few times with a fork. This is done to prevent the (albeit uncommon) aubergine from exploding during cooking.
2. Barbecue straightforwardly on a gas fire until totally consumed and darkened all through and delicate in the center, turning sometimes. Depending on the size and shape of the aubergines, this can take anywhere from ten to twenty minutes. See text above for different choices.)
3. Peel the skin off when it is cool enough to handle. This is either simple or erratic at times. Whatever it is, don't be alarmed if there are still a few small pieces of burned skin. It will only enhance the smoky flavor.
4. To prevent long, stringy pieces, cut the flesh of the aubergine in a few random places. Mash with a fork until the texture is just right. I like it a little chunkier.
5. Salt and the remaining ingredients should be added. Tahini, lemon juice, or salt can all be added to taste. Serve at room temperature, embellished with additional virgin olive oil and pomegranate seeds or new mint, contingent upon what's in season and accessible.

# ZELJANICA (CHEESE & SPINACH PIE)

Prep Time: 25 Minutes

Cook Time: 45 Minutes

Servings: 9-12 Peoples

## INGREDIENTS

- vegetable oil, for the tin
- 4 medium eggs
- 500g curd cheese, crumbled (this can be found in specialist shops), or use 250g ricotta mixed with 250g mascarpone
- 250g feta, crumbled
- 2 tbsp soured cream
- 500g frozen spinach, defrosted and excess moisture wrung out in a clean tea towel
- 100ml olive oil
- 300ml natural yogurt
- 1 tsp baking powder
- 500g filo pastry
- 20g unsalted butter

## INSTRUCTIONS

1. Line a roasting tin with baking parchment and lightly oil it—ours was about 25 x 35 cm and 4 cm deep. In a bowl, combine the eggs, cheeses, spinach, soured cream, and some seasoning.
2. Combine the oil, yogurt, and baking powder in another bowl. Turn on the oven to 200°C/180°C fan/gas 6.
3. Divide the filo sheets in half to make them about the same size as a tin. Put one filo sheet in the tin and uniformly brush north of 1-2 tbsp of the yogurt combination utilizing baked good brush. Brush more yogurt mixture over the top of the filo, then repeat until you've used half of the sheet.
4. Use a spatula to spread the cheese filling out gently to the edges. Layer the remaining yogurt mix and filo sheets as usual. The final filo sheet should be covered with any yogurt mix that is still present.
5. Divide the pie into nine or twelve squares, depending on the size you want for the pieces. will keep for up to a month in the freezer. Before cooking, defrost completely overnight in the refrigerator. Bake for 20 minutes, then top each square with a small knob of butter. Bake another 25 to 30 minutes, uncovered, at 180C/160C fan/gas 4, until browned on top. Allow to slightly cool before serving hot. will keep for up to two days covered and chilled.

# SYRIAN BABA GANOUSH

Prep Time: 10 minutes

Cook Time: 25 minutes

Passive Time: 5 minutes

Servings: 3-4 servings

## INGREDIENTS

- 2 large aubergines
- 1 garlic clove, crushed to a paste with a little salt
- 1 small tomato, finely chopped
- 2 Tbsp finely chopped flat-leaf parsley
- 1 1/2 Tbsp chopped walnuts
- 2 Tbsp pomegranate molasses
- 1 Tbsp lemon juice
- salt and pepper

## INSTRUCTIONS

1. Using a fork, poke the aubergines in a few places. Burn, turning occasionally, for 10-15 minutes or more over a direct flame or near a hot grill until soft inside and completely burned out on the outside. Peel the burned skin when it is cool enough to handle and throw it away.
2. Mix the remaining ingredients together after cutting the aubergine crosswise a few times to avoid long strings. Add more pomegranate molasses or herbs to taste and season to taste with salt and pepper. The dish can be prepared a few hours ahead and kept covered until serving.

# QUICK SALMON, PRESERVED LEMON & OLIVE PILAF

Prep Time: 10 Minutes

Cook Time: 30 Minutes

Servings: 4 Servings

## INGREDIENTS

- 240g brown rice
- 500ml vegetable stock
- 4 boneless and skinless salmon fillets
- 1 tsp ground cinnamon
- 1 tsp ground cumin
- 1 tsp turmeric
- 1 preserved lemon from a jar, skin finely chopped, flesh and seeds discarded
- 130g pitted green olives, sliced
- small pack parsley, roughly chopped

## INSTRUCTIONS

1. Cover the rice with the vegetable stock and bring to a boil in a saucepan. Cover and cook for 15 minutes at a simmer after it has reached boiling point. Remove the lid and let the rice sit for 15 minutes without turning off the heat.
2. The salmon fillets should be covered with cling film and placed on a plate that can be heated in the microwave. Cook until just cooked in the microwave on high for four minutes. Stir in the spices, preserved lemon, olives, parsley, and a little seasoning when the rice is ready. Serve the salmon by flaking it and gently mixing it into the rice without breaking it up too much.

# TABBOULEH WITH POMEGRANATE

Prep Time: 5-10 Minutes

Cook Time: 20 Minutes

Servings: 4-6 Servings

## INGREDIENTS

- 25 g fine bulgur
- 150 g cherry tomatoes or other very good sun-ripened tomato, finely chopped
- 2 Tbsp lemon juice
- 200 g flat-leaf parsley, thick stalks removed, finely chopped (c. 85 g net weight)
- 25 g mint, leaves only, finely chopped
- 2-3 spring onions, finely chopped or 1/2 red onion, finely chopped
- 1/2 large pomegranate, seeds only
- 1 Tbsp pomegranate molasses
- 2 Tbsp extra virgin olive oil
- lettuce leaves (gem lettuce is perfect), to serve
- salt and pepper

## INSTRUCTIONS

1. Combine the bulgur, tomato, lemon juice, and a pinch of salt. Set aside for 5 to 10 minutes or until the bulgur becomes soft. Chop the herbs in the meantime.
2. Combine the bulgur, tomato, onion, and herbs in a bowl. Once more, add pomegranate molasses and additional virgin olive oil and blend. Season.
3. Use small lettuce leaves as bowls to serve immediately, or serve in a bowl with lettuce leaves on the side.

# SLOW COOKER LAMB TAGINE

Prep Time: 20 Minutes

Cook Time: 4 Hours

Servings: 4 Servings

## INGREDIENTS

- 900g lamb shoulder, neck or leg, cut into chunks
- 1 tbsp olive oil
- 1 onion, chopped
- 3 carrots, cut into chunks
- 2 tsp ras-el-hanout
- 1 tsp ground cumin
- 1 tbsp tomato purée
- 1 chicken or lamb stock cube or stock pot
- 1 sweet potato, cut into chunks
- 30g dried cherries
- ½ tsp honey
- ½ bunch coriander, chopped
- couscous, to serve

## INSTRUCTIONS

1. Broil the sheep in the oil in clusters and tip it into the sluggish cooker. In the same pan, fry the onion for 5 minutes, or until it begins to soften. Stir in the spices, carrots, tomato purée, 250 milliliters of water, and stock before moving everything around the pan. Incorporate into the slow cooker. Add the yam, dried cherries, honey and another 500ml water.
2. Cook for 8 hours on low or 4 hours on high. Serve with couscous and stir in the coriander. Before freezing, allow to cool.

# SPICED BEETROOT AND CHICKPEAS WITH HARISSA YOGHURT

Preparation Time : 10 Minutes

Cook Time: 30 Minutes

Servings : 4-6 People

## INGREDIENTS

- 3 Tbsp olive oil
- 4 medium beetroots (c. 700-800 g), peeled and cut into large chunks
- 1 Tbsp za'atar, plus more to garnish
- 1 Tbsp sumac
- ½ tsp Urfa pepper (isot biber) or Aleppo pepper (pul biber)
- 10-15 mint leaves, finely sliced
- salt and pepper

### HARISSA YOGHURT:

- 400 g yoghurt, preferably greek style
- 2 Tbsp lemon juice
- 2 Tbsp harissa

### CHICKPEAS:

- 3 Tbsp olive oil
- 250 g boiled chickpeas (from 100 g dried, soaked equivalent to 1×400 g tin, drained)
- 1 tsp ground cumin
- ½ tsp paprika
- salt and pepper

## INSTRUCTIONS

1. Heat both the top and bottom of the oven to 220 C.
2. Add three tablespoons of olive oil, za'atar, sumac, salt, and pepper to the beetroot mixture. Depending on the size of the chunks, bake for approximately 30 minutes after spreading on a roasting tray. I cut the beets down the middle, then, at that point, I cut every half into four pieces.
3. By combining the yoghurt, harissa, and lemon juice, you can make harissa yoghurt. Season.
4. Chickpeas should be fried in the remaining 3 tablespoons of olive oil until hot, starting to color, and starting to crisp up on the outside. Add the paprika and cumin, and cook for an additional minute. Remove the intensity and season with salt and pepper if essential (tinned chickpeas will quite often be adequately pungent as of now).

5. Spread the harissa yogurt on a serving plate and orchestrate the beetroot and chickpeas on top. Add some additional za'atar, chili flakes, and mint leaves for decoration.

## BAHARAT BAKED CHICKEN THIGHS

Prep Time: 20 minutes

Cook Time: 40-45 minutes

Passive Time: 5 minutes

Servings: 4-6 servings

## INGREDIENTS

- 1 pound baby potatoes, halved
- 3 large shallots, halved, and cut into thick slices
- 8 boneless skinless chicken thighs, about 1.5 pounds
- Kosher salt
- 3 tablespoons sesame seeds, toasted
- Parsley for garnish

**For The Marinade:**

- Juice of 2 to 3 limes
- ½ cup extra virgin olive oil
- 10 to 15 garlic cloves, minced
- 4 tablespoons tomato paste
- 2 teaspoons Baharat
- ½ teaspoon to 1 teaspoon red pepper flakes

## INSTRUCTIONS

1. Preheat the oven to 425 degrees Fahrenheit and place a rack in the middle of the oven.
2. Get the marinade ready. Add the Baharat, red pepper flakes, olive oil, garlic, lime juice, and tomato paste to a large mixing bowl. Combine by mixing.
3. Add kosher salt to the potatoes and toss them with about 1 cup of the marinade mixture. Place the potatoes and shallots in the bottom of a 9"x13" cast iron pan that has been lightly oiled.
4. Place the potatoes and shallots in a baking pan on the center rack of your heated oven. Bake for one hour.
5. In the meantime, pat the chicken dry and sprinkle it with kosher salt on both sides. Add the chicken to the mixing bowl and toss it around until the marinade is evenly distributed over it. Set aside about fifteen minutes.

6. Add the sesame seeds to a small skillet that has been heated to medium-high. Toss frequently until the seeds start to turn a light shade. This won't take much time. Sesame seeds consume effectively, so don't leave them unattended. Once toasted, set aside.
7. Place the chicken in between the potatoes and shallots after carefully removing the baking pan from the oven. Return the baking container to the stove and cook for around 30 minutes or until the chicken is completely cooked through.
8. After the chicken has been removed from the heat, garnish it with toasted sesame seeds and parsley. Enjoy!

## SIMIT BREAD

Prep Time: 30 minutes

Cook Time: 15 minutes

Servings: 4 servings

## INGREDIENTS

- 250g strong white bread flour
- 1 tsp salt
- 1 tsp caster sugar
- 1 tsp (5g) fast-action dried yeast
- 100g sesame seeds
- 1 tbsp pomegranate molasses or molasses syrup

## INSTRUCTIONS

1. Mix together the flour, sugar, and salt in a bowl. Mix in the 150 milliliters of warm water and the yeast before kneading for a few minutes to form a soft dough. Place the dough on a work surface and continue to knead for 10 to 12 minutes, or until it feels stretchy. Cover and return to a clean bowl for an hour or two until doubled in size.
2. In the meantime, toast the sesame seeds until golden in a dry frying pan. Put the pan aside for now. In a large, shallow bowl, combine 50 milliliters of water with the pomegranate molasses or molasses syrup.
3. The dough should be cut into four equal pieces. Roll each one into a sausage about 45 centimeters long. To secure the dough rope, fold it back over itself and twist the two loops into a ring by squeezing the ends together. Once formed, dunk each piece into the molasses water, going to cover, then into the sesame seeds, it is very much covered to ensure every one. Cover and place on a baking sheet to prove for an additional 45 to 1 hour. Pre-heat the oven to 200 C/180 C fan/gas 6.

4. At the point when the breads have puffed up, uncover them and heat for 15-18 mins until brilliant. Wrap them in a tea towel once cool to keep them fresh. It can be prepared up to a day in advance and warmed gently before being served.

## **TARATOR-STYLE SALMON**

Prep Time: 10 minutes

Cook Time: 15 minutes

Servings: 4 servings

## INGREDIENTS

- 50g walnuts, finely chopped
- large handful parsley leaves, finely chopped
- 2 tsp sumac, see 'Tip' below
- ½ red onion, finely chopped
- zest and juice 1 lemon
- 4 salmon fillets
- 2 tbsp hummus
- couscous, pitta bread or flatbreads, to serve (optional)
- yogurt, to serve (optional)

## INSTRUCTIONS

1. Pre-heat the oven to 200 C/180 C fan/gas 6. Combine the chopped walnuts, sumac, parsley, red onion, lemon zest, and half the lemon juice in a bowl. Season gently and put away.
2. After roasting for 12 minutes on a baking sheet, spread the salmon with hummus and return it to the oven for another 3 minutes. Serve with couscous, pita, or flatbreads, and, if desired, yogurt on the side, along with the remaining lemon half for squeezing over the top.

# CHICKEN WITH POMEGRANATE & BRAZIL NUTS

Prep Time: 35 minutes

Cook Time: 45 minutes

Servings: 6 servings

## INGREDIENTS

### For Chicken:

- 150g pack Brazil nuts, half left whole, half chopped
- thumb-sized piece ginger, peeled
- 1 garlic clove
- juice 1 lime
- 250g pot of coconut milk yogurt (we used Coyo Natural)
- 4 tbsp pomegranate molasses
- 6 free-range chicken legs or quarters

### To Serve:

- 2 tbsp rapeseed oil
- 2 large aubergines, sliced lengthways
- 1 pomegranate, seeds only

## INSTRUCTIONS

1. In a food processor, combine the ginger, garlic, and lime juice with the whole Brazil nuts. Add the molasses and coconut yogurt after blending to a paste. Tip into a large bowl with the chicken after briefly blending to combine. Cover the bowl with cling film and refrigerate for the night to coat it thoroughly in the marinade.
2. Heat oven to 190C/170C fan/gas 5 the next day. Cook the chicken, skin-side down, in a deep roasting tin for 45 to 1 hour, or until golden brown and the juices run clear.
3. Brush the aubergine slices with the oil while the chicken is cooking and cook them on a hot griddle pan for 3 to 4 minutes on each side, or until they are tender and have char marks on them. On a serving platter, arrange the aubergines, cooked chicken, and chopped Brazil nuts and pomegranate seeds.

## MIDDLE EASTERN CARROT SALAD

Preparation Time : 15 Minutes

Cooking Time : No Need

Servings : 4 servings

### INGREDIENTS

- ½ tsp orange blossom water
- ½ tsp ground cumin
- 1 tbsp extra virgin olive oil
- juice ½ lemon
- 500g carrot, shredded or grated
- large handful small mint leaves

### INSTRUCTIONS

1. Put the orange bloom water, cumin, oil, lemon juice and some flavoring into a container. Attach the lid and vigorously shake to combine.
2. Place the mint and carrots in a bowl. Season and toss everything together after pouring over the dressing.

## BAKLAVA

Prep Time: 40 minutes

Cook Time: 1 hour and 5 minutes

Servings: make 25-28 pieces

### INGREDIENTS

- 200g butter, plus extra for greasing
- 200g pistachios
- 50g walnuts
- 50g pecans
- 3 tbsp honey
- 2 x 270g pack filo pastry
- For the syrup
- 250g golden caster sugar
- 50g honey
- 2 tsp orange blossom water
- ½ tsp ground cinnamon
- ¼ tsp ground cardamom (from 3 pods)

## INSTRUCTIONS

1. Butter-grease a square cake pan measuring 21 cm x 21 cm and preheat the oven to 180 C/160 C fan/gas 4. Using a food processor, chop the nuts into small pieces without blitzing them into a paste. Put them in a bowl, add some salt and honey, and set it aside.
2. In a pan, melt the butter over low heat. Divide the first package of filo pastry sheets in half (to fit the tin). Brush one sheet with the melted butter after placing it in the tin. Place a second sheet on top and brush it with butter once more. Continue layering in this manner until the entire pack is used up.
3. Using the back of a spoon, lightly press the honey and nut mixture onto the pastry. Open the other pack of filo, cut down the middle and proceed with the layering and buttering process. Pour any remaining butter over the top of the last sheet to finish. Utilize a sharp blade to cut profound lines into the cake to make either squares or jewel shapes then prepare in the broiler for 20 mins.
4. Diminish the intensity to 150C/130C fan/gas 2 and prepare for a further 45 mins. Put all of the ingredients for the syrup in a saucepan and add 200 milliliters of water while the baklava is cooking. After gently heating the mixture until the sugar has dissolved, boil it for 8 to 10 minutes, or until it has the consistency of runny honey.
5. Pour the warm syrup over the top of the baklava as soon as it comes out of the oven, allowing it to run along the lines you cut. Serve it when it is completely cold, allowing it to soak in.

# SPICY HARISSA PASTA

Prep Time: 10 minutes

Cook Time: 30 minutes

Servings: 4 servings

## INGREDIENTS

- ¾ cups cashews
- 1 red bell pepper
- 400 g spaghetti pasta
- 1 onion
- 2 garlic cloves
- 2 ½ tablespoon harissa paste
- lemon juice from ½ lemon
- 200 ml vegetable stock or water
- A handful pistachios
- 3-4 sun-dried tomatoes preserved in oil
- A handful fresh oregano

## INSTRUCTIONS

1. Preheat the oven to 200 C (400 F). 2. Combine the cashews and boiling water in a small bowl. Allow to soak for approximately 20 minutes. Rinse, drain, and put aside.
2. While the cashews are soaking, wash the red pepper, place it in a small baking dish or casserole, poke a few tiny holes in the skin with a knife or fork, and bake for about 30 minutes, or until the skin is charred.
3. Leave to cool and eliminate the skin and seeds.
4. You can cook the pasta according to the package instructions while the cashews are soaking and the red pepper is roasting. To cook the pasta al-dente, use salted water and save some of the pasta water for later.
5. Reserve the pasta after draining it and coating it with olive oil to prevent sticking.
6. Heat some olive oil in a little container over medium intensity, and add the onion finely hacked.
7. Stir and cook it until it becomes soft. After that, add the finely sliced garlic and cook it for another 3 to 4 minutes before turning off the heat.
8. Add to a blender container the splashed cashews, the cooked red pepper, sautéed garlic and onion, harissa glue, lemon juice, and vegetable stock or water.
9. Blend until the cashews are completely incorporated and the sauce is smooth.
10. Add crushed pistachios, finely chopped sun-dried tomatoes, and fresh oregano or parsley to the pasta and sauce in a pan.
11. Mix thoroughly, add any remaining pasta water if necessary, and serve.

## RECIPE NOTES

I. We like using some of the pasta water if we need to reheat the dish after a few hours of making it to get that creamy sauce again.
II. To make this dish milder, use half of the Harissa paste listed. If you want the dish to be spicier, add more Harissa paste.
III. Serve with some crusty bread, a fresh salad, or some roasted veggies.

## MOROCCAN VEGETABLE TAGINE

Prep Time: 15 minutes

Cook Time: 1 hour

Servings: 4-5 servings

## INGREDIENTS

- 3 medium-size potatoes
- 1 red onion
- 3 carrots
- ½ aubergine
- 1 red pepper
- 2 tomatoes
- ½ can chickpeas
- 1 preserved lemon
- 1 cup black olives
- ¼ cup dried apricots
- 500 ml hot water or vegetable stock
- 1 ½ teaspoon Ras el Hanout
- 1 ½ teaspoon turmeric
- 1 teaspoon cumin seeds
- ½ teaspoon chili flakes optional to make this dish mildly spicy
- 1 teaspoon salt
- 1 teaspoon olive oil

**Ingredients for the Tahini Sauce:**

- ½ cup tahini
- 2 tablespoon lemon juice
- Water

## INSTRUCTIONS

1. Preheat the oven to 150C or 300F (fan-assisted oven).
2. Peel and slice the potatoes into 1cm thick slices (about ½ inch).
3. Peel the onion, cut it in half, and finely slice it.
4. Peel the carrots, and slice them in half or quarters depending on the size.
5. Slice the aubergine into 1cm thick slices (about ½ inch).
6. Cut the bell pepper into big chunks and cut the tomato into big wedges.
7. Place the vegetables into the tagine pot creating layers.
8. Rinse and add the canned chickpeas to the tagine.
9. Add the preserved lemon finely chopped and the black olives. Finely chop the dried apricots and add to the pot.
10. Using a kettle or a pan, bring water to a boil. Pour the hot water into a jug and mix in the Ras el Hanout, turmeric, cumin seeds, chili flakes, and salt.
11. Pour the broth into the tagine, add a dash of olive oil, and cover with the lid.
12. Leave cooking for 1 hour at 150C (300F) without opening the lid.
13. Serve the tagine with bread or couscous and tahini sauce on the top.

**Tahini Sauce**

1. To prepare the tahini sauce, mix in the tahini with the lemon juice, and salt, and keep adding cold water until desired consistency. Whisk the mixture until there are no lumps and you have a creamy sauce. For serving on top of the veggies, we like the consistency to be creamy and quite thick.

# ARABIC LENTIL SOUP

Prep Time: 5 minutes

Cook Time: 25 minutes

Servings: 4-6 servings

## INGREDIENTS

- 1 medium onion finely chopped
- 1 garlic clove minced
- 2 carrots finely chopped
- 1 celery stalk finely chopped
- 1 tomato
- 1 teaspoon ground cumin
- ½ teaspoon ground coriander
- ¼ teaspoon ground cinnamon
- ¼ teaspoon turmeric
- 1 cup red lentils rinsed and picked over
- 4 cup vegetable broth
- ¼ cup chopped fresh cilantro
- Salt and pepper to taste
- Lemon to serve

## INSTRUCTIONS

1) Heat some olive oil in a major pot over medium intensity. Cook for 2 to 3 minutes before adding the onion.
2) Tomato, carrot, celery, and finely chopped garlic should be added. Cook for seven to ten minutes while stirring frequently.
3) Add spice mix and red lentils. Stir well and cook for 1-2 minutes.
4) Bring the vegetable stock to a simmer and cook the lentils for 20 minutes, or until they are fully cooked.
5) Add salt and pepper to taste.
6) Using an immersion blender or hand blender, half blend the soup or blend until you have the desired consistency.
7) Serve with lemon drizzle and chopped parsley or coriander.

# TURKISH EGGS (CILBIR)

Prep Time: 15 minutes

Cook Time: 10 minutes

Servings: 2 servings

## INGREDIENTS

- 1 cup Greek yoghurt
- Few fronds fresh dill
- 8-10 mint leaves
- ½ garlic clove
- 2 eggs
- 1 tablespoon vinegar
- 55 g butter
- 1 teaspoon chili flakes
- ½ teaspoon smoked paprika
- Salt and pepper to taste

## INSTRUCTIONS

1) Crush or grate the garlic clove, finely chop the dill and mint, and combine the ingredients with the Greek yogurt. Add salt and pepper to taste, and set aside.
2) Bring boiling water to a boil in a large pot. A vortex will form when one tablespoon of vinegar is added. The egg should be cracked and placed in the center of the vortex. Cook for three minutes to get the ideal egg with a runny yolk. Use a slotted spoon to remove the egg and set it aside while the next egg is cooked.
3) Butter must be melted in a pan. Add the spices when the butter starts to bubble. The sauce will be ready to serve when it has been thoroughly mixed.
4) Place the Greek yogurt in the bowl for serving. The chili sauce should be poured over the eggs. On top, sprinkle some additional dill and mint.

# ROASTED CAULIFLOWER SALAD WITH TAHINI DRESSING

Prep Time: 15 minutes

Cook Time: 30 minutes

Passive Time: 5 minutes

Servings: 4 servings

## INGREDIENTS

- 1 cauliflower head medium size
- 2 cups chickpeas
- 3 tablespoon olive oil
- 2 teaspoon za'atar
- 1 teaspoon cumin
- 1 teaspoon coriander
- 1 teaspoon smoked paprika
- 50 g rocket salad
- 100 g baby spinach
- ½ pomegranate
- 1 avocado
- 5-6 fresh mint leaves
- Sumac add to taste before serving

**Tahini Dressing**

- 2 garlic cloves
- A pinch of salt
- 4 tablespoon tahini
- 2 tablespoon lemon juice
- Water Add slowly while whisking until desired consistency

## INSTRUCTIONS

1) Pre-heat the oven to 400°F (200°C).
2) Add chickpeas and a cauliflower head cut into florets to a large mixing bowl. Combine the salt, za'atar, cumin, coriander, sweet paprika, and olive oil until the cauliflower and chickpeas are thoroughly coated. Depending on the size of your cauliflower, you can always adjust by adding more spices or oil.
3) Bake the chickpeas and cauliflower together on a baking sheet for 25 to 30 minutes, or until the chickpeas are crispy and the cauliflower is tender and golden. To ensure that everything is cooking evenly, make sure to stir the ingredients halfway through.
4) You can begin assembling your salad once your cauliflower and chickpeas are prepared. Before adding them to the salad bowl, let them cool for a few minutes to keep the leaves

fresh. Add the baked cauliflower and chickpeas, spinach, rocket, pomegranate, avocado, finely chopped fresh mint, sumac, and some additional Za'atar to taste for a delicious lemony flavor.

# FALAFEL PITA SANDWICH

prep Time: 40 minutes

Cook Time: 10 minutes

Servings: 20 falafels

## INGREDIENTS

- 2 cups dried chickpeas
- 4 garlic cloves finely chopped
- 1 small onion finely chopped
- 1 cup broccoli florets
- ¾ cups fresh coriander chopped
- ½ cup parsley chopped
- 1 teaspoon coriander powder
- 1 teaspoon cumin powder
- 1 teaspoon black pepper
- 1 teaspoon salt add more to taste

**Ingredients for the Falafel Sandwich**

- Pita bread
- Hummus
- 1 large tomato
- ½ cucumber
- Green or black olives
- Sambal or hot sauce optional

## INSTRUCTIONS

1) Leave the chickpeas soaking overnight, at least 12 hours before preparing your falafels.
2) Once your chickpeas have been soaking for at least 12 hours, rinse them and remove the excess of water. Add them in a food processor and blend for a couple of seconds.
3) Add to the food processor the onion, broccoli, fresh coriander, fresh parsley, coriander powder, cumin powder, black pepper and salt.
4) Blend all the ingredients until you have a well-combined mixture. It shouldn't be mushy as the balls will be too dense, but it needs to be blended enough for the dough to not fall apart when frying them.

5) Using your hands or using a falafel press, form the dough into round shapes. Make sure the size is not too small or too big. It should be around the size of your palm.
6) Heat up some neutral oil in a small frying pan so you don't have to use that much oil. Fry the falafels until they are brown and crispy on the outside. If the falafels are shaped correctly, not much oil will go inside. The inside part will still be really fresh and light.
7) Cut the Pita Bread in half, spread some hummus and spicy sauce (optional) on the bread, add some fresh chopped tomatoes and cucumber drizzled with some olive oil, add lettuce and finally the homemade falafels. Top the sandwich with green or black olives. Optionally, can add some yoghurt sauce as well.

## VEGAN CHARCUTERIE BOARD

Prep Time: 1 hour and 30 minutes

Servings: 4-6 servings

### INGREDIENTS

- Baba Ganoush
- Roasted Carrot Hummus
- Sun-Dried Tomato Pate
- Edamame Hummus
- Tomato Chutney
- Vegan Cream Cheese
- Grapes
- Raspberries
- Blueberries
- Cherry Tomatoes
- Cucumber
- Red and Green Apple
- Kiwi
- Walnuts
- Dried Apricots
- Dates
- Raisins
- Roasted Almonds
- Olives

### INSTRUCTIONS

1) Make the dips. You can find the recipes for each dip on our website. We left all the links on the post above. Keep them in the fridge until you start making the board.

2) Choose the board you will be serving the charcuterie items on. Adjust the board size to the amount of people that this will be served to. Place the pinch bowls where the dips will be served so you know where to start adding the rest of the ingredients.
3) Start by adding the fresh fruits. Our board contains blueberries, raspberries, kiwi, cucumber, tomatoes and grapes. We add apple too, but at the end to avoid oxidation. You can add any fruits or veggies you want. Raw carrots, celery sticks, strawberries or blackberries are lovely options too.
4) Add the dried fruits and nuts. On our board you will find dried apricots, walnuts, olives, almonds, raisins and dates.
5) Fill up the pinch bowls with the dips. We use Baba Ganoush, Sun-Dried Tomato Pâté, Roasted Carrot Hummus, Tomato Chutney, Vegan Cream Cheese and Edamame Hummus.
6) Fill the empty spaces with an assortment of crackers and sliced apples. We like using a red and a green apple for colour contrast.

## SPICED CAULIFLOWER ROAST

prep time : 20 minitues

Cook Time: 40 minutes

Servings: 4-6 servings

## INGREDIENTS

- 50g butter, softened at room temperature
- 2 tsp chilli flakes
- ½ tsp sumac
- ½ tsp allspice
- 1 tsp ground cumin
- 1 tsp ground coriander
- 1 cauliflower (about 1kg)
- 2 x 400g cans chickpeas, drained and rinsed
- small pack flat-leaf parsley, chopped
- small pack mint, chopped
- small pack coriander, chopped
- 1 red onion, very finely chopped
- 200g cherry tomatoes on the vine
- 50g pine nuts, toasted
- pomegranate molasses, for drizzling
- For the feta dressing
- 100g good-quality feta

- 100g Greek yogurt
- juice ½ lemon

## INSTRUCTIONS

1) In a little bowl, beat the margarine and flavors with a wooden spoon, then, at that point, put away.
2) Turn the oven on to 220C/200C fan/gas 7. The outer leaves of the cauliflower should be cut off, and the very bottom of the root should be taken out. Be careful to keep some of the root attached so that the whole cauliflower stays in its original shape. Bring salted water to a rolling boil in a large pan large enough to hold the entire cauliflower. To partially tenderize, cook for 3 to 4 minutes, then carefully remove with two slotted spoons.
3) Place the chickpeas and cauliflower on a baking sheet. Rub the cauliflower with the spread, dab a little over the chickpeas and season everything. Roast for 35 minutes, or until a knife can easily be inserted into the middle of the cauliflower and the chickpeas are crispy and deep golden brown.
4) Make the feta dressing in the meantime. Whisk the feta and Greek yogurt together in a large bowl until the cheese is completely broken down and the mixture is creamy. Whisk once more before adding the lemon juice. Season to taste. Chill until required.
5) Mix the remaining ingredients, with the exception of the pomegranate molasses, with the warm chickpeas on the tray after removing the cauliflower and chickpeas from the oven.
6) Place the whole cauliflower on top of the herby chickpeas on a large serving platter. Spoon over the dressing and shower with pomegranate molasses to serve.

# MUHAMMARA WITH ROASTED CAULIFLOWER, QUINOA AND HALLOUMI

Prep Time: 15 minutes

Cook Time: 60 minutes

Servings: 2 servings

## INGREDIENTS

- 2 Italian peppers
- 35 g walnuts
- 35 g breadcrumbs
- 2 tablespoons extra virgin olive oil
- 1 teaspoon aleppo pepper chilli flakes
- ½ teaspoon smoked paprika
- 1 garlic clove
- 1 teaspoon lemon juice
- 1 teaspoon maple syrup
- 1 teaspoon cumin
- ¼ cauliflower head
- 1 teaspoon sweet paprika
- 1 tablespoon olive oil
- Salt and pepper to taste
- 2 tablespoon raisins
- Quinoa
- 1 block halloumi
- Chopped mint
- Pommegranate
- Olive oil
- Lemon juice

## INSTRUCTIONS

1) Preheat the stove to 200C°. Broil the Italian peppers for around 25 minutes or until the skin has darkened.
2) Remove the skin from the peppers and allow them to cool. Since the cauliflower will be cooked in the oven, keep it on. Add the walnuts, breadcrumbs, olive oil, chili flakes, smoked paprika, garlic, lemon juice, maple syrup, and cumin to a food processor.
3) Blend all of the ingredients until they have a consistency that is even and smooth.
4) Bake the cauliflower for about 30 minutes after cutting it into small florets, coating it with olive oil and sweet paprika. Add raisins to the baking sheet and bake them along

with the cauliflower for an additional 15 minutes after the cauliflower has been in the oven for 10 minutes. Remove the baking sheet from the oven and set it aside.
5) To cook the quinoa, use a 1:2 ratio, which means that you should use twice as much water for the quinoa and cook it without covering the pan. At the point when all the water has vanished, your quinoa will be all set.
6) Grill the halloumi until golden on a skillet pan after cutting it into slices.
7) Place the cooked quinoa in the middle of the plate, topped with the roasted cauliflower and raisins, and then add the Muhammara sauce to the side of the plate. Final step: sprinkle the Halloumi on top. Add chopped mint, pomegranate, and olive oil and lemon juice to the garnish.

## ROASTED RED PEPPER HUMMUS

Prep Time: 10 minutes

Cook Time: 15 minutes

Servings: 4 servings

## INGREDIENTS

- 1 Italian red pepper
- 500 g chickpeas cooked
- 1-2 garlic cloves crushed
- ¼ cup tahini
- Juice of half a lemon
- 1 tsp smoked paprika
- 1 tbsp olive oil
- Salt to taste

## INSTRUCTIONS

1) The pepper should be roasted for ten minutes in the oven, or until it is completely soft. Place it in a sealed container after it has been cooked. Leave it in while the remaining ingredients are prepared. Use jarred roasted red pepper instead.
2) Add the chickpeas to the food processor after draining and rinsing them. Salt, smoked paprika, tahini, lemon juice, and crushed garlic should be added.
3) Add the red pepper to the food processor after removing the skin.
4) Blend everything together until the mixture is smooth. If it's too thick, add a little cold water and keep adding it little by little until you get the right consistency.
5) Serve drizzled with extra virgin olive oil or chilli oil and refrigerated for at least 10 minutes.

# WHOLE WHEAT PITA BREAD

Prep Time: 20 minutes

Cook Time: 2 hours

Servings: 6 pitas

## INGREDIENTS

- 165 gr all-purpose flour
- 165 gr wholewheat flour
- 212 ml lukewarm water
- 17.5 gr fresh yeast
- ¾ tsp salt

## INSTRUCTIONS

1) In a large bowl, combine the whole wheat and white flours. Mix the fresh yeast with the water in a jug until it is completely dissolved. Add the salt to the flour, add the water and yeast mixture, and knead the dough by hand for about ten minutes.
2) For one hour, or until the dough has doubled in size, cover it with a damp tea towel.
3) Get rid of all the air in the dough. It was weighed and cut into six equal pieces.
4) Cover the dough for an additional hour before rolling it into balls.
5) Using a rolling pin, roll the balls into balls.
6) Bake for three to four minutes at the highest setting in the oven.

# BEETROOT CARPACCIO

Prep Time: 5 minutes

Cook Time: 1 hour 15 minutes

Servings: 4 servings

## INGREDIENTS

- 1 medium-size beetroot
- ½ medium-size pear
- A handful of lamb's lettuce or rocket salad
- A handful of walnuts
- 2 tablespoons extra virgin olive oil
- 1 tablespoon apple cider vinegar
- 6 leaves mint finely chopped
- ½ tablespoon lime
- 1 teaspoon maple syrup
- 1 teaspoon mustard
- Salt

## INSTRUCTIONS

1) Cut the top and bottom off of a fresh beetroot, wash it, and wrap it in tin foil before putting it in the oven at 200 C/400 F.
2) If you are using pre-cooked beetroot, skip this step and bake for approximately one hour and fifteen minutes at 200 degrees Celsius. Once heated, pass on to cool.
3) Place the beetroot on the serving plate after being thinly sliced. Add the salad with rocket.
4) Place the pear shavings on top of the beetroot after shaving them into small pieces.
5) Mix olive oil, apple cider vinegar, mustard, maple syrup, fresh mint leaves, and a pinch of salt to make the vinaigrette. Wisk every one of the fixings together until consolidated. Pour over the salad leaves and beetroot.
6) Squash a few pecans and sprinkle on top prior to serving.

# LEBANESE POUSSIN WITH SPICED AUBERGINE PILAF

prep. time : 15 minutes

Cook Time: 45 minutes

Servings: 4 servings

## INGREDIENTS

- 1 aubergine, roughly diced
- 1 tbsp olive oil, plus a bit extra
- 2 small poussin
- ¼ tsp allspice, plus 2 good pinches
- 2 bay leaves
- 1 onion, halved and thinly sliced
- 100g basmati rice
- 2 tbsp pine nut
- ½ tsp ground cinnamon
- good pinch of ground cloves
- 200ml hot chicken stock (or gluten-free alternative)
- 2 tbsp currant
- 1 large tomato, chopped
- 1 tbsp chopped mint, plus a few leaves and sprigs to serve
- 1 tbsp chopped dill, plus a few leaves and sprigs to serve
- 2 tbsp pomegranate molasses
- sumac, for sprinkling (optional- we used Bart)

## INSTRUCTIONS

1) Turn the oven on to 200°C/180°C fan/gas 4. Toss the aubergine well in 1 tablespoon of the oil. Push the mixture to the sides of a large roasting pan to create a space for the poussins. Rub some oil onto the skin of the poussins, sprinkle with the portions of allspice, salt and heaps of dark pepper, pop an inlet leaf inside each bird, then cook for 35 mins. ( Before beginning the pilaf, allow it to cook for about 10 minutes so that both are ready at the same time.)
2) In a medium pan, heat the remaining 1 tbsp oil and fry the onion until golden for 5 to 8 minutes to make the pilaf. Stir in the rice and pine nuts for about a minute before adding the spices, including the one-fourth teaspoon of allspice. Cover the pan, add the stock, stir in the currants, and cook for seven minutes.
3) Remove the lid, add the tomato, dill, and mint, and cover the pan to cook another 2-3 minutes until the rice is tender and the stock has been absorbed. Cover and place aside to keep warm.

4) In the meantime, after the poussins have been in the oven for 35 minutes, drizzle them with the pomegranate molasses and return them to the oven for another ten minutes, or until the poussins and aubergines are tender.
5) Put the poussins to the side to rest for a couple of mins while you throw the aubergine into the pilaf. The poussins can be served whole or portioned and placed on top of the pilaf. Sprinkle with the mint and dill leaves and, if you like, a little sumac.

## GRILLED AUBERGINES WITH SPICY CHICKPEAS & WALNUT SAUCE

Prep Time: 20 minutes

Cook Time: 30 minutes

Servings: 2 servings

### INGREDIENTS

- 4 tbsp olive oil
- 1 onion, finely chopped
- 1 red chilli, deseeded and finely chopped
- 2cm piece ginger, finely chopped
- ½ tsp each ground cumin, coriander and cinnamon
- 400g can chickpeas, rinsed and drained
- 200g tomatoes, chopped
- juice ½ lemon
- 2 aubergines, sliced lengthways
- 200g tub Greek-style yogurt
- 1 garlic clove, crushed
- 25g walnuts, chopped
- handful coriander leaves, roughly chopped

### INSTRUCTIONS

1) In a pan, heat 2 tablespoons of oil. Add the onion and fry for about 10 minutes until soft and lightly browned. Mix thoroughly the spices, ginger, and chilli. Bring the water to a boil and stir in the chickpeas, tomatoes, and 5 tablespoons of water. Simmer for 10 minutes. Sprinkle a little salt, pepper, and lemon juice on top.
2) Over a grill pan, arrange the aubergines. Grill until golden, sprinkle with salt and pepper, and lightly brush with oil. Again brush them with oil, season, and grill until tender and golden on the other side.
3) Combine the yogurt, coriander, the majority of the walnuts, the garlic, and a little salt and pepper. Spread the chickpea mixture over the aubergine slices and arrange them on

a warm platter. Sprinkle with the remaining walnuts and coriander and drizzle with the walnut sauce.

## HERBY QUINOA, FETA & POMEGRANATE SALAD

prep time : 10 minutes

Cook Time : 15 minutes

Passive Time : 30 minutes

Servings : Serves 4 or 6-8 as a side

### INGREDIENTS

- 300g quinoa
- 1 red onion, finely chopped
- 85g raisins or sultana
- 100g feta cheese, crumbled
- 200g pomegranate seeds from tub or fruit
- 85g toasted pine nuts or toasted flaked almonds
- small pack each coriander, flat leaf parsley and mint, roughly chopped
- juice 3 lemon
- 1 tsp sugar

### INSTRUCTIONS

1) Follow the package's instructions to cook the quinoa until it is tender but still slightly firm. Spread out on a platter or wide, shallow bowl to steam dry after being thoroughly drained.
2) Stir in all of the remaining ingredients with plenty of seasoning when the quinoa is just about cool.

# LAMB & APRICOT MEATBALLS

Cook Time: 30 minutes

Servings: 4-6 servings

## INGREDIENTS

- 2 tbsp olive oil
- 2 red onions, very finely chopped
- 4 garlic cloves, crushed
- 2 tsp each ground cumin and coriander (or 4 tsp Moroccan spice blend)
- 400g can chopped tomatoes
- ½ tsp sugar
- ½ 20g pack mint, finely chopped
- 500g pack lean lamb mince
- 8 dried apricots, finely chopped
- 50g fresh breadcrumbs
- pitta bread and salad, to serve

## INSTRUCTIONS

1) Heat 2 tsp oil painting in a visage and soften the onions for 5 minutes. Add the garlic and spices and cook for a many minutes more. ladle half the onion admixture into a coliseum and set away to cool. Add the tomatoes, sugar and seasoning to the remaining onions in the visage and poach for about 10 minutes until reduced.
2) Meanwhile, add the mint, angel, apricots and breadcrumbs to the cooled onions, season and mix well with your hands. Shape into little meatballs.
3) Toast the rest of the oil painting in anon-stick visage and fry the meatballs until golden( in batches if you need to). Stir in the sauce with a splash of water and gently cook everything for a many minutes until the meatballs are cooked through. Serve with pitta chuck and salad.

# MIDDLE EASTERN BREAD & GOAT'S CHEESE SALAD

Cook Time: 20 minutes

Passive Time: 15 minutes

Servings: 4 servings

## INGREDIENTS

- 2 pitta breads
- 1 garlic clove
- juice 1 lemon
- 3 ripe plum tomatoes, cut into chunks
- 1/2 cucumber, cut into chunks
- 6 radishes, sliced
- 1 small red onion, halved and sliced
- large handful mint leaves, very roughly chopped
- 1 small Cos lettuce, roughly chopped
- 1 Baby Gem lettuce, roughly chopped
- 2 large handfuls rocket
- 5 tbsp olive oil
- 200g firm goat's cheese, crumbled into large chunks

## INSTRUCTIONS

1) Cook the pitta chuck on a griddle or in a toaster oven until brown and crisp. When cool enough to handle, tear into bite- size pieces.
2) Mash the garlic clove with a pinch of swab, also tip into a large coliseum and stir in the bomb juice. cock all the other constituents, except the olive oil painting and scapegoat's rubbish, into the coliseum, also dapple over the oil painting. Gently toss everything together until mixed and dressed.
3) Serve the salad in piles with scapegoat's rubbish atrophied over each serving.

# LAMB & APRICOT STEW

Prep Time: 10 minutes

Cook Time: 35 minutes

Servings: 2 servings

## INGREDIENTS

- 2 tbsp olive oil
- 250g stewing lamb pieces
- 1 onion, thinly sliced
- 1 garlic clove, chopped
- 1 tbsp chopped ginger
- 2 tsp ras-el-hanout, Berber or other Middle Eastern spice mix
- 1 tbsp tomato purée
- 5 soft dried apricots, halved
- 300ml vegetable or chicken stock
- cooked couscous, mint or coriander leaves, and lemon wedges, to serve

## INSTRUCTIONS

1) In a medium-sized pan, heat 1 tbsp of the oil. Season the meat and fry briefly until browned. Remove from the pan and add the remaining oil.
2) Add the onion, garlic and ginger, and fry with a little seasoning.
3) Cook for 5 mins until soft, then add the spice mix, tomato purée, apricots and stock, and return the lamb to the pan.
4) Simmer gently for 25 mins.
5) Serve with warm couscous, mint or coriander leaves, and lemon wedges.

# FALAFEL BURGERS

Prep Time: 10 minutes

Cook Time: 6 minutes

Servings: 4 servings

## INGREDIENTS

- 400g can chickpeas, rinsed and drained
- 1 small red onion, roughly chopped
- 1 garlic clove, chopped
- handful of flat-leaf parsley or curly parsley
- 1 tsp ground cumin
- 1 tsp ground coriander
- ½ tsp harissa paste or chilli powder
- 2 tbsp plain flour
- 2 tbsp sunflower oil
- toasted pitta bread, to serve
- 200g tub tomato salsa, to serve
- green salad, to serve

## INSTRUCTIONS

1) Clean the chickpeas off with kitchen paper after draining them. Place the onion, garlic, parsley, cumin, coriander, harissa paste, flour, and a small amount of salt in a food processor.
2) Shape four patties with your hands after you have blended until they are fairly smooth.
3) In a nonstick frying pan, heat sunflower oil and fry the burgers for three minutes on each side until lightly golden.
4) Tomato salsa, green salad, and toasted pitta bread are all great accompaniments.

# TURKISH LAMB FLATBREAD

Prep Time: 45 minutes

Cook Time: 25 minutes

Servings: 6-8 servings

## INGREDIENTS

- 1 tsp dried yeast
- 400g plain flour, plus extra for dusting
- 1 tsp salt
- a little oil
- semolina, for dusting
- For the spicy lamb topping
- 500g lean lamb leg meat, finely chopped (or lean mince)
- 1 tbsp olive oil
- 1 onion, finely chopped
- 2 garlic cloves, finely chopped
- 2 tsp Turkish chilli flakes or 1tsp chilli flakes
- 2 tsp ground cumin
- 2 tsp ground cinnamon
- 4 tbsp tomato purée
- 400g can plum tomatoes, drained
- 4 tbsp pomegranate molasses, plus extra for drizzling
- 2 small red onions, thinly sliced into half moons
- 50g pine nuts
- 100g feta, crumbled
- 2 tbsp chopped flat-leaf parsley
- 50g pomegranate seeds

## INSTRUCTIONS

1) Blend the yeast and 250ml warm water in a little bowl, and pass on to represent 5-10 mins until frothy - this implies the yeast is working.
2) Alternatively, you can use a tabletop mixer with a dough hook and low speed to combine the flour and salt. Mix in the yeast mixture by hand or with a machine until the dough forms a ball. If the mixture is too sticky to form a ball, mix it again with 2 tablespoons of flour. Massage for 12 mins manually, or 8-10 mins on a rapid in the blender, until smooth, then put in a softly oiled bowl.
3) Cover the dough with cling film and turn it over to coat it in the oil. Leave it in a warm place for two to four hours until it has doubled in size. You can also punch it down and let it rise again at room temperature after putting it in the refrigerator overnight.)

4) Turn on the oven to 240°C/220°C/gas 9.
5) Place a pizza stone or baking sheet on the middle shelf. In the event that you're utilizing sheep leg meat, barrage it in a food processor until it's finely minced. In a large frying pan, heat the olive oil until it is hot over medium-high heat. Cook for 10 minutes, until the onion and garlic are golden.
6) After adding the lamb and cooking for five minutes, stirring to break up any lumps, drain any excess oil. Cook for an additional 5 minutes, stirring everything thoroughly and breaking down the tomatoes with a spoon, before adding the spices, some seasoning, tomato purée, tomatoes, and pomegranate molasses.
7) Eliminate from the intensity and pass on to totally cool. can be done ahead of time one or two days.
8) Carry out the mixture on a floured surface into a huge square shape around 30 x 40cm. On a baking sheet, sprinkle the semolina with about a teaspoon. Make sure the dough can move around before placing it on top.
9) The red onions, pine nuts, and feta are then added on top of the spicy lamb. Slide onto a heated baking sheet or pizza stone, and cook for 10 to 15 minutes until the bottom is crisp.
10) Sprinkle the parsley and pomegranate seeds over the dish after removing and drizzling with some extra pomegranate molasses.
11) Divide into diamonds and transfer to a large board for serving.

# FATTOUSH SALAD

Prep Time: 15 minutes

Servings : 2-3 servings

## INGREDIENTS

- 2 tomatoes, chopped into chunks
- ¼ cucumber, deseeded and sliced
- ½ red onion, sliced
- 1 small head romaine lettuce, shredded
- handful mint leaves, roughly chopped
- handful parsley leaves, roughly chopped
- 2 pitta breads
- 1 tsp sumac
- ½ garlic clove, crushed
- 2 tbsp red wine vinegar
- 1 tbsp extra virgin olive oil
- juice ½ lemon

## INSTRUCTIONS

1) Mix all of the salad ingredients, with the exception of the pitta bread and sumac, the night before. Make up the dressing and season to taste. These should be kept apart until the morning.
2) Toast the pitta breads until lightly golden the following morning. Divide into bite-sized pieces once cool, and combine with the salad and dressing. Spoon into 2 plastic boxes and sprinkle over the sumac.

# SLOW-ROAST PERSIAN LAMB WITH POMEGRANATE SALAD

Prep Time: 20 minutes

Cook Time: 3 hours and 30 minutes

Servings: 6 servings

## INGREDIENTS

### For the lamb

- 4 tbsp pomegranate molasses
- 1 tsp ground cumin
- juice 1 lemon
- 1 tbsp olive oil
- 2 garlic cloves, minced
- 1 onion, roughly chopped
- 1 shoulder of lamb, weighing about 1.6kg, lightly scored

### For the Salad

- seeds 2 pomegranates
- handful flat-leaf parsley leaves
- 100g bag watercress
- 1 small red onion, finely diced
- 1 tbsp olive oil
- flatbreads, to serve

## INSTRUCTIONS

1) Heat oven to 160C/140C fan/gas 3. In a small bowl, mix the molasses with the cumin, lemon juice, olive oil and garlic. Scatter the onion over a casserole dish or a deep roasting tin. Place the lamb on top of the onions. Pour the glaze over the lamb. Rinse the bowl out with about 200ml water, then pour it around – not over – the lamb.
2) Cover the dish with a lid or the tin with a large piece of foil. Roast the lamb, undisturbed, for 3 hrs, then remove the lid or foil and continue to roast for 30 mins to give the lamb colour. When the lamb has had its time, pour off the juices, remove as much fat as possible, then pour the juices back over the lamb.
3) Just before serving, gently toss all the salad ingredients together. Serve the lamb with its sauce, the salad and some warmed flatbreads.

# MIDDLE EASTERN EGGS WITH MERGUEZ & PISTACHIOS

Prep Time: 10 minutes

Cook Time: 25 minutes

Servings: 2 servings

## INGREDIENTS

- drizzle of olive or rapeseed oil
- 1 small red onion, chopped
- 4 merguez sausages
- 15 cherry tomatoes, halved
- pinch of sugar (any will do)
- 2 tsp harissa paste (preferably rose harissa, as it's fragrant and not too hot)
- 2 eggs
- 2 wholemeal pitta breads
- pinch of sumac or paprika (optional)
- 2 tbsp Greek yogurt
- few parsley sprigs, chopped
- 1 tbsp shelled pistachio, roughly chopped

## INSTRUCTIONS

1) Heat a shower of oil in a weighty lined, little skillet - a cast-iron one is great. After the onion has softened, add it and cook for a few minutes before moving it to one side of the pan. Roll the sausages around in the pan until they are golden brown before adding them and frying for 5 to 10 minutes. Season to taste, add a splash of water, and add the tomatoes, sugar, and harissa. Cook, stirring occasionally, for 5 to 10 minutes until the tomatoes have reduced to a thick, chunky sauce.
2) Put the sausages aside in the pan so that you can use a spoon to make two big holes in the sauce. Place the eggs in the holes and cook for 4-5 minutes, or until the yolk is still runny and the whites are just set. In the interim, toast the pitta breads.
3) Sprinkle a little sumac over each egg, top with yogurt, and then top with parsley and pistachios. Serve each pitta bread cut in half on the side.

# MANAKEESH

Prep Time: 30 minutes

Cook Time: 10 minutes

Servings: 4 servings

## INGREDIENTS

- lavash or wholemeal khobez flatbreads (see tips)
- 200g pack feta

**For the Turkish salad**

- good-quality tomatoes, chopped into rough cubes
- ½ cucumber, chopped into rough cubes
- ½ small pack mint, leaves picked and torn
- 15 pitted black olives
- balsamic vinegar, for drizzling
- extra virgin olive oil, for drizzling

**For the garlic yogurt**

- 1 garlic clove, crushed
- 150ml pot natural or Turkish yogurt

**For the za'atar dressing**

- ½ small pack oregano
- bunch thyme, leaves picked
- 150ml olive oil
- garlic cloves, crushed
- juice 0.5 lemon
- ¼ tsp sumac
- sesame seeds, toasted

## INSTRUCTIONS

1) Make the salad first. In a large bowl, combine the olives, tomato, cucumber, and mint with a little balsamic vinegar and extra virgin olive oil. Season to taste.
2) Season and set aside after thoroughly mixing the yogurt with the crushed garlic.
3) Blend the garlic, olive oil, oregano, and thyme in a jug with a stick blender to make the dressing. Stir in the sumac, sesame seeds, lemon juice, and some seasoning.
4) Spread two heaping tablespoons of the za'atar dressing on one side of each flatbread, and then top each with a quarter of the feta.

5) Crease the flatbreads down the middle or roll up and gently fry each on the two sides in a dry iron skillet over a medium intensity until softly toasted and brilliant. Keep warm in the oven on a low heat while you fry the other things.
6) Serve with a heaping helping of the Turkish salad and some garlic yogurt on top.

## ZA'ATAR

Prep Time: 5 minutes

Cook Time: 2 minutes

Servings: 6-8 servings

### INGREDIENTS
- 2 tbsp cumin
- 2 tbsp sesame seeds
- 2 tbsp dried oregano
- 2 tbsp sumac

### INSTRUCTIONS
1) In a dry pan, lightly toast the cumin seeds until they begin to release their aroma.
2) Using a pestle and mortar, crush them into a fine powder. Add all the other ingredients, plus 2 teaspoons of salt and 1 teaspoon of freshly ground black pepper.
3) It is presently prepared to use in your recipes, however will save in a spotless container or impenetrable compartment for a month.

# SPICY BABY AUBERGINE STEW WITH CORIANDER & MINT

Prep Time: 10 minutes

Passive Time: 45 minutes

Servings: 4 servings

## INGREDIENTS

- 2 tbsp olive oil
- 2 red onions, sliced
- 4 garlic cloves, smashed
- 2 red chillies, deseeded and sliced, or 2-3 dried red chillies left whole
- 2 tsp coriander seeds, toasted and crushed
- 2 tsp cumin seeds, toasted and crushed
- 16 baby aubergines, left whole with stalk intact
- 2 x 400g cans chopped tomatoes
- 2 tsp sugar
- bunch mint leaves, roughly chopped
- bunch coriander, roughly chopped
- couscous and yogurt to serve

## INSTRUCTIONS

1) In a heavy-bottomed saucepan, heat the oil, add the garlic, and cook the onions and garlic until they begin to brown. Chili, coriander, and cumin seeds should be added. Toss the whole aubergines with the onion and spices when the seeds start to smell nutty.
2) Cover and cook for 40 minutes, stirring occasionally, until aubergines are tender. Add tomatoes and sugar.
3) Add half of the mint and coriander to the sauce and season it. Cover and stew for 2 mins. Serve with couscous and yogurt and sprinkle with the remaining herb.

# FAMILY MEALS: EASY LAMB TAGINE

Prep Time: 10 minutes

Cook Time: 2 hours and 30 minutes

Servings: 4-6 servings

## INGREDIENTS

- 2 tbsp olive oil
- 1 onion, finely diced
- 2 carrots, finely diced (about 150g)
- 500g diced leg of lamb
- 2 fat cloves garlic, crushed
- ½ tsp cumin
- ½ tsp ground ginger
- ¼ tsp saffron strands
- 1 tsp ground cinnamon
- 1 tbsp clear honey
- 100g soft dried apricot, quartered
- 1 low-salt vegetable stock cube
- 1 small butternut squash, peeled, seeds removed and cut into 1cm dice
- steamed couscous or rice, to serve
- chopped parsley and toasted pine nuts, to serve (optional).

## INSTRUCTIONS

1) In a heavy-based pan, add the onion and carrot to the olive oil. Cook for 3-4 mins until relaxed.
2) Brown all over the diced lamb when you add it. Mix in the garlic and every one of the flavors and cook for a couple of mins more or until the fragrances are delivered.
3) Crumble the stock cube into the honey and apricots, add 500 milliliters of boiling water to cover the meat, and serve. Give it a thorough stir before bringing to a boil. Reduce the heat to a simmer, cover, and cook for one hour.
4) Stir in the squash after 30 more minutes of cooking after removing the lid. The lamb should be tender and the squash soft after another 20 to 30 minutes of cooking. Serve close by rice or couscous and sprinkle with parsley and pine nuts, if utilizing.

# PISTACHIO LAMB KOFTAS WITH APRICOT RELISH

Prep Time: 20 minutes

Cook Time: 20 minutes

Servings: 4 servings

## INGREDIENTS

- 2 ½ tbsp olive oil
- 3 red onions, 2 1/2 thinly sliced, 1/2 grated
- 400g lamb mince
- 1 tbsp ras el hanout
- 85g pistachios, roughly chopped
- ½ small pack flat-leaf parsley, roughly chopped
- 4 tbsp good-quality apricot jam
- zest and juice 1 lemon
- 2 carrots, cut into skinny matchsticks
- 4 round wholemeal pitta breads, split and warmed
- 4 tbsp Greek-style yogurt, to serve

## INSTRUCTIONS

1) In a frying pan, add 1 1/2 tbsp olive oil, most of the sliced onions, and season with salt and pepper. Cook for about 15 minutes, until soft and golden.
2) Set the grill to high while you wait. Mix the mince, grated onion, ras el hanout, the majority of the pistachios, half of the parsley, and some seasoning in a large bowl. Form patties from the mixture divided into eight portions. Brush with half a tablespoon of oil and place on a baking sheet. Cook, turning once, for approximately 10 minutes until browned and cooked through.
3) Add the apricot jam, a huge spot of zing and a portion of the lemon juice to the cooked cut onions, bubble down until thick, then put away. To make the plate of mixed greens, blend the carrots, saved cut onions and remaining parsley in a bowl, then throw in the leftover lemon juice and olive oil and some flavoring. Scoop the apricot relish into the pittas before serving. The remaining pistachios, yogurt, and koftas should now be added. Alternately, serve the pittas open and loaded with filling.

## HERB SALAD WITH POMEGRANATE & PISTACHIOS

Prep Time: 15 minutes

Servings: 6 servings

## INGREDIENTS

- juice 1 orange
- 3 tbsp red wine vinegar
- 1 tbsp clear honey
- small bunch dill, very roughly chopped
- small bunch mint, picked and torn
- bunch spring onions, finely sliced
- 100g bag mixed salad leaves
- 120g tub pomegranate seeds (or seeds from 1 pomegranate)
- 100g bag pistachios, roughly chopped

## INSTRUCTIONS

1) Season with the juice, vinegar, and honey.
2) To serve, combine the remaining ingredients in a large mixing bowl, drizzle with the dressing, and gently toss.

## BUTTERNUT & HARISSA HUMMUS

Prep Time: 10 minutes

Cook Time: 45 minutes

Servings: 6 servings

## INGREDIENTS

- ½ butternut squash (about 400g), peeled and cut into 2cm pieces
- 3 garlic cloves, unpeeled
- 2 tbsp olive oil
- 3 tbsp tahini paste
- 1 tbsp harissa, plus a little extra for drizzling
- 400g can chickpeas, drained and rinsed

## INSTRUCTIONS

1) Pre-heat the oven to 200 C/180 C fan/gas 6. Season the butternut squash and garlic cloves thoroughly before adding 100 milliliters of water to a roasting tin. Bake for 45 minutes, covered with foil, until the squash is very tender. Allow to cool.
2) Put the squash and any juices from the tin into a food processor. Remove the garlic from its skins and add it. Blend the remaining ingredients into a paste and season with salt.
3) Place the hummus in a bowl with a spoon. Before serving, drizzle with extra harissa.

## HARISSA ROAST SALMON WITH LEMON CHICKPEA COUSCOUS

Prep Time: 30 minutes

Cook Time: 50 minutes

Servings: 8-10 servings

## INGREDIENTS

### For the salmon

- 2 tbsp olive oil
- 2 large onions, halved and thinly sliced
- 1 large fennel bulb, halved and thinly sliced
- 1 garlic clove, chopped
- 1 tsp cumin seeds
- zest 1 lemon
- 2 tbsp harissa
- 1 tbsp agave nectar or clear honey
- 2 x 1kg/2lb 4 oz boneless sides of salmon, skin removed

### For the couscous

- 1 vegetable stock cube
- 2-3 tsp harissa
- 50g currants
- 300g couscous
- 2 x 400g cans chickpeas, drained
- juice 2 lemons, zest of 1
- 2 tbsp olive oil
- big bunch flat-leaf parsley, chopped
- small bunch mint, chopped (optional)
- 50g toasted flaked almonds
- lemon wedges, to serve

## INSTRUCTION

1) Heat the oil in a large non-stick frying pan, add the onions, fennel, garlic and cumin seeds and fry, stirring frequently, for about 15 mins until the vegetables are soft and golden.
2) Stir in the lemon zest and season. Leave to cool. After covering the vegetables in an even layer, place the second salmon fillet on top, placing its thickest end on top of its thinnest end. can be prepared up to this point by covering and chilling overnight.
3) With a large baking sheet inside, heat the oven to 200 C/180 C fan/gas 6. After brushing the salmon with the remaining harissa mixture, transfer it to the hot baking sheet while still on the parchment and bake for 30 minutes.
4) Verify that the fish has fully cooked after taking it out of the oven; If it is not done to your liking, cook an additional five minutes and check again. Crumble the stock cube into a large bowl and add the harissa, currants, and couscous to make the couscous. In the meantime, combine the chickpeas, oil, and seasoning in a bowl.
5) Pour 450 milliliters of boiling water over the couscous just before serving, stir well, cover with a plate, and let it soak for five minutes.
6) After thoroughly mixing in the lemon zest, parsley, and mint (if using), toss the chickpeas with the hot couscous and flaked almonds.
7) Serve on a major, warm platter with the salmon (the simplest method for moving the salmon is to lift it still on the material, then slide it on top), with lemon wedges as an afterthought. Slice the salmon into thin slices to serve, or cut it in half to make chunky squares.

# ROAST AUBERGINE WITH GOAT'S CHEESE & TOASTED FLATBREAD

Prep Time: 15 minutes

Cook Time: 20 minutes

Passive Time: 5 minutes

Servings: 2 serving

## INGREDIENTS

- 2 aubergines, thinly sliced lengthways
- 3 tbsp extra-virgin olive oil
- 12 cherry tomatoes, halved
- 1 Middle Eastern flatbread or pitta
- 3 tbsp balsamic vinegar
- handful mint leaves
- 2 shallots, 1 finely chopped, the other thinly sliced
- 1 red chilli, finely chopped
- 50g goat's cheese, crumbled
- handful wild rocket, to serve

## INSTRUCTIONS

1) Pre-heat the oven to 200 C/180 C fan/gas 6. Season the aubergine slices after brushing them with 1 tablespoon of the oil. Place the tomatoes on a baking sheet or tray and roast for 20 minutes until they are browned, putting them back on the tray for the last 5 minutes. Tear the flatbread into pieces and put on a different baking sheet. Remove after eight minutes of crisping in the oven.
2) Mix the vinegar, mint, chopped shallots, chilli, remaining oil, salt, and pepper in a small bowl to make the dressing.
3) Disperse the aubergine cuts, tomatoes, cut shallot and fresh flatbread into a serving bowl. Pour over the dressing, sprinkle with the goat's cheddar and dissipate over a little rocket.

# HERBY COUSCOUS WITH CITRUS & POMEGRANATE DRESSING

Prep Time: 15 minutes

Passive Time: 5 minutes

Servings: 4 servings

## INGREDIENTS

- 200g couscous
- 5 150g pack pomegranate seeds
- handful chopped herbs (we used mint and coriander)
- juice 1 orange
- 2 tbsp each white wine vinegar and olive oil

## INSTRUCTIONS

1) Pour 200 milliliters of boiling water over the couscous after placing it in a shallow bowl. Leave the bowl covered with cling film for five minutes, or until the couscous has expanded and absorbed all of the water. After separating the grains with a fork, stir in the pomegranate seeds and herbs.
2) Make a dressing by combining as one the squeezed orange, white wine vinegar and olive oil, then mix into the couscous. Add salt to taste and serve.

# CHICKEN WINGS WITH CUMIN, LEMON & GARLIC

Cook Time: 10 minutes

Passive Time: 50 minutes

Servings: 6 serving

## INGREDIENTS

- 12 chicken wings
- 2 garlic cloves, crushed
- zest and juice 1 lemon
- 1 tsp cumin seed
- 2 tbsp olive oil
- 1 tbsp honey

## INSTRUCTIONS

1) Utilizing some sharp kitchen scissors, cut each wing at the knuckle into two pieces. Add the chicken wings to a dish and toss to coat with the oil, cumin, lemon zest and juice, and plenty of seasoning. Cover and marinate for at least one hour, or overnight if you have time, in the refrigerator.
2) Either heat an outdoor barbecue or heat an oven to 200C/180C fan/gas 6. Heat the chicken wings on a stove plate for 45-50 mins until fresh, or grill for 20 mins, showering over the honey for the last 10 mins of every strategy. Serve on a platter with a lot of paper napkins. Fill little dishes with olives, pistachios or almonds, dates and salted chillies and flatbreads to serve close by, alongside the dishes underneath.

# SWEET POTATO SALAD

Cook Time: 15 minutes

Passive Time: 35 minutes

Servings: 6 servings

## INGREDIENTS

- 1.2kg sweet potato, peeled and cut into biggish chunks
- 1 tbsp olive oil
- For the dressing
- 2 shallots (or half a small red onion), finely chopped
- 4 spring onions, finely sliced
- small bunch chives, snipped into quarters or use mini ones
- 5 tbsp sherry vinegar
- 2 tbsp extra-virgin olive oil
- 2 tbsp honey

## INSTRUCTIONS

1) Pre-heat the oven to 200 C/180 C fan/gas 6. Throw the yam pieces with the olive oil and some flavoring, and spread on a baking material lined baking sheet. Cook for 30 - 35 mins until delicate and brilliant. At room temperature, cool.
2) Use your hands to avoid breaking up the potato chunks as you gently toss them through the dressing once it is almost completely cool. Season to taste.

# LENTIL KOFTA WITH ORZO & FETA

Cook Time: 25 minutes

Passive Time: 30 minutes

Servings: 4 servings

## INGREDIENTS

- 2 x 400g cans cooked green lentils, drained
- 1 medium egg
- 100g oat
- 1 tbsp ras el hanout
- small bunch parsley, chopped
- zest 1 lemon
- 2 tbsp olive or rapeseed oil
- 4 garlic cloves, crushed
- 2 x 400g cans chopped tomatoes
- pinch of sugar
- 300g orzo pasta
- 100g feta, crumbled

## INSTRUCTIONS

1) In a food processor, combine the lentils, egg, oats, ras el hanout, half the parsley, and lemon zest. Blitz in some seasoning until it is finely chopped. After removing the blade, form the mixture into cherry tomato-sized balls and chill for 20 minutes. Pre-heat the oven to 200 C/180 C fan/gas 6.
2) In the mean time, heat 1 tbsp of the oil in a container. After 30 seconds of sizzling the garlic, add the tomatoes, sugar, and some seasoning. The sauce should bubble for 20 to 25 minutes until it's rich and thick. While the sauce cooks, line a baking plate with foil and orchestrate the kofta on top. Sprinkle with the remaining oil, bake for 20 minutes, rolling the tray around halfway through. Once cooked, add the kofta to the pureed tomatoes, tenderly covering every one.
3) Following the package's instructions, cook the orzo, drain it, and divide it among four plates. Sprinkle the remaining parsley on top of the crumbled feta, top with the sauce and kofta, and serve.

# SMOKY AUBERGINE & CORIANDER DIP

Prep Time: 10 minutes

Cook Time: 20 minutes

Servings: 10 servings

## INGREDIENTS

- 4 large aubergines
- 4 tbsp Greek yogurt
- 2 tbsp olive oil
- large bunch coriander, leaves only, finely chopped
- 1 garlic clove, crushed
- squeeze lemon or lime juice

## INSTRUCTIONS

1) Lay the aubergines, two to a ring, directly on top of the gas on two rings. Use tongs to turn them until they are well charred on all sides, as they will have blackened on one side in 30 seconds. Alternately, cook the aubergines, turning them occasionally, until they are all blackened, either on the barbecue or under the grill.
2) Put the aubergines in a plastic bag when you're done. Remove the blackened skin when it is cool enough to handle and place the cooked and soft flesh in a colander to drain for 30 minutes.
3) Move the aubergine to a bowl, then, at that point, crush with a fork or barrage with a hand blender, yet don't make it totally smooth. Mix in the yogurt, olive oil and a fat spot of salt, then, at that point, add coriander, garlic and lemon or lime juice. Taste and adjust as necessary with more salt or lemon juice, taking care not to overpower the aubergine's flavor.

# LEBANESE CHICKEN WRAPS

prep time : 20 minutes

cook time : 10 minutes

Servings : 4 servings

## INGREDIENTS

- 4 skinless chicken breasts
- 200g Greek yogurt
- juice and zest 1 lemon
- 1 tsp allspice
- 2 tsp olive oil
- 2 garlic cloves, crushed
- 25g pine nuts, toasted
- small bunch parsley, finely chopped
- 2 tomatoes, diced
- ½ cucumber, diced
- 4 large tortilla wraps or large flatbreads
- mixed salad, to serve

## INSTRUCTIONS

1) Cover the chicken breasts with another sheet of baking parchment and flatten them by rolling them with a rolling pin. Blend a portion of the yogurt in an enormous bowl with a portion of the lemon squeeze, the lemon zing, allspice, olive oil, garlic and a spot of salt. After thoroughly combining the ingredients, add the chicken, making sure it is thoroughly coated. To marinate, cover and chill for 30 minutes.
2) Cook the chicken on each side in a griddle pan over high heat for 5 to 6 minutes, or until cooked through (you may need to do this in batches). Slice after transferring to a board. Fill the wraps with the pine nuts, cooked chicken, parsley, tomatoes, and cucumber after spreading the remaining yogurt over them. Roll up and drizzle the remaining lemon juice over it. Serve the wraps with a mixed salad after being lightly toasted for 30 seconds on each side on the griddle pan.

# AUBERGINE & GOAT'S CHEESE SALAD WITH MINT-CHILLI DRESSING

Prep Time: 15 minutes

Cook Time: 25 minutes

Servings: 4 servings

## INGREDIENTS

- 2 aubergines
- 1 tbsp extra-virgin olive oil
- 2 pieces lavash bread or pitta bread
- 175g cherry plum tomato, halved or quartered
- 4 large handfuls salad leaves
- 2 shallots, thinly sliced
- 50g hard goat's cheese
- For the mint-chilli dressing
- 3 tbsp balsamic vinegar
- 2 tbsp extra-virgin olive oil
- 1 large handful mint leaves, finely chopped
- 1 red chilli, seeds removed, finely chopped
- 1 shallot, finely chopped

## INSTRUCTIONS

1) Heat broiler to 200C/180C fan/gas 6. Slice the aubergine into 3 cm-wide pieces. Sprinkle with olive oil and season. Roast for 25 minutes, or until browned, on a baking sheet.
2) Place the bread in pieces on a baking sheet and bake. Place the bread in the oven and bake for 8 minutes, just as the aubergine is getting close to being ready.
3) Combine all of the ingredients for the mint-chilli dressing in a small bowl and season. The remaining dressing can be used to drizzle over the salad. Toss the aubergine with about one third of the dressing. On a large platter, arrange the tomatoes, salad leaves, shallots, dressed aubergine, and crisp bread. Sprinkle the saved dressing over and disperse the goat's cheddar on top.

# HALVA

Prep Time: 5 minutes

Total Time: 3 hours and 30 minutes

Passive Time: 15 minutes

Servings: 20 servings

## INGREDIENTS

- 1 1/2 c. tahini
- 3/4 tsp. kosher salt
- 1 1/2 c. granulated sugar
- 1/3 c. water
- 1/2 vanilla bean (or 1 tsp pure vanilla extract)

### FOR CARDAMOM PISTACHIO HALVA

- 3/4 c. toasted pistachios
- 1/2 tsp. cardamom

### FOR CHOCOLATE SWIRLED HALVA

- 3 oz. roughly chopped chocolate

### FOR COFFEE HALVA

- 1/4 c. strong coffee

## INSTRUCTIONS

1) Using parchment paper, line an 8-by-8-inch pan. In a large bowl, combine the salt and tahini. Under the bowl, place a kitchen towel to make stirring easier.
2) Combine the sugar, water, and seeds of the vanilla bean in a medium saucepan over medium heat. Add vanilla extract to the tahini mixture if you are using it. Give it a stir, and then bring the mixture to 245° without stirring. Utilize a wet cake brush to wipe drawbacks of skillet as sugar gems structure.
3) Whenever blend is warmed to 245°, cautiously and gradually empty syrup into tahini combination while blending and keep on mixing until completely joined and combination thickens. After it has thickened, be careful not to overmix, or your halva will be too crumbly.
4) Fill the pan with the mixture and smooth the top. Refrigerate for at least three hours until chilled to room temperature.
5) To the tahini mixture, add cardamom. Stir in 12 cups of pistachios after adding the sugar mixture to the tahini.

6) Fill the prepared pan with the mixture, top it with the remaining 14 cup of pistachios, and refrigerate for at least 3 hours until chilled.
7) After incorporating the sugar mixture into the tahini, add the chocolate to the bowl and allow it to sit for thirty seconds. Stir in the chocolate slowly, leaving streaks.
8) Refrigerate for at least three hours after pouring into the pan that has been prepared.
9) Combine the coffee and salt in the tahini by stirring.
10) Heat the sugar mixture and add it as directed.

## KNAFEH NA'AMEH

Prep time : 40 minutes

Cook Time: 15 minutes

passive time : 2 hours

Servings: 4-6 serving

## INGREDIENTS

### FOR THE SCENTED SUGAR SYRUP:
- 2 cups (400g) granulated sugar
- 1 cup (230g) water
- Squeeze of lemon
- 2 teaspoons orange blossom water (more or less to taste)
- 1/2 teaspoon rose water (more or less to taste)

### FOR THE CHEESE FILLING:
- 500g Shellala/Meshalela cheese (preferably without black sesame)
- 300g Akkawi Tchiki Cheese

### FOR THE KNAFEH CRUST (FARKEH):
- 375g kunafa (aka kataifi dough), fresh or frozen
- 1/3 cup plus 2 tablespoons (94g) melted ghee (or clarified butter *instructions below)
- 3 tablespoons (60g) scented sugar syrup
- 3 tablespoons (45g) water
- 2 tablespoons (30g) ghee or clarified butter, at room temperature, for cooking the knafeh
- Ground pistachios, for garnish (optional)

## INSTRUCTIONS

1) Combine the sugar, water, and a squeeze of lemon juice in a medium saucepan. Set on the burner over medium high intensity. To prevent crystallization, try not to stir it as it

heats, but if the sugar isn't dissolving, give it a few stirs to help it along. STOP stirring when it reaches a boil.

2) After bringing to a boil, immediately turn down the heat to low and allow it to simmer for no more than ten minutes. Put in a timer! The consistency of the syrup will slightly thicken and resemble that of warm pancake syrup. If it simmers for a longer period of time, it may become candy-like and impossibly thick. Add the rose and orange blossom water by stirring.

3) Move to a medium bowl or sauce pitcher and permit to cool to room temperature prior to utilizing.

4) Thinly slice the shelal and akkawi cheeses with a sharp knife. Cover each kind of cheese in its own bowl with lukewarm tap water to get rid of the salt. Permit the cheddar to drench for 2 to 6 hours, changing the water each 1/2 hour, until the cheddar is as of now not pungent to the taste. Measure of splashing time will fluctuate contingent upon the cheddar's salt substance, which is the reason they are put in discrete bowl. The cheese bowls should be kept in the refrigerator while this step is completed overnight.

5) Squeeze the two cheeses with your hand or the back of a spoon to remove any excess liquid before draining them through a colander. Disintegrate the two cheeses along with your hands or in food processor to consolidate equitably. Put away in the colander to deliver any abundance dampness, as you set up the knafeh outside (farkeh).

6) (can be made ahead of time and frozen) Process the kunafa in batches in a spice grinder until it is very finely ground and powdery. It ought to be like fine bread crumbs in texture. Move to a medium bowl and mix in the ghee, 3 tablespoons of scented sugar syrup and water until very much joined and homogenous. It should feel very damp, look like cooked couscous, and stick to itself when squeezed between your palms.

7) Combine the shredded kunafa strands, ghee, three tablespoons of the scented sugar syrup, and water in a medium bowl until the kunafa is thoroughly coated. Go through a meat processor until a clumpy combination emerges from the opposite side.

8) Place the kunafa mixture in a large, medium-sized skillet. The kunafa mixture should be toasted, stirring frequently to prevent browning, until it no longer sticks to itself and feels dry and sandy. The color ought to get darker by one shade. Transfer to a food processor to smooth out any lumps while it is still hot, or strain through a large mesh sieve. The farkeh can be frozen for months in a zipper-lock bag at this point.

9) Only use the two tablespoons of room-temperature ghee to brush a 34-cm aluminum or copper pan. Eliminate 3 tablespoons of the farkeh and put away. Sprinkle the remaining farkeh evenly over the pan's bottom and use your hand to compact it into a compact, even layer about 3/4 cm thick.

10) Cover the knafeh crust with the cheese mixture, leaving a 2 cm border uncovered.

11) Make sure that only half of the pan's bottom is lit by placing it over one side of the stovetop. The center of the knafeh will burn before the sides have a chance to cook if the pan is centered over the stovetop. In the event that utilizing an electric oven, set the intensity to medium high; Set your gas stove to medium heat. Involving utensils in a single hand and wearing broiler gloves in the other, turn the skillet consistently for

baking, tapping the cheddar with a perfect material or kitchen towels to retain any delivered dampness. Keep rotating the pan until the cheese is mostly melted and the crust's edge is deep golden brown; ten to fifteen minutes You can tell by the crust's edge; The actual color of the knafeh's bottom is whatever color it is. Take the pan off the heat.

12) Cover the dish and let rest for a couple of moments to permit the cheddar to liquefy the whole way through. To prevent the cheese from sticking to the serving platter and to absorb any excess moisture, sprinkle the remaining three tablespoons of farkeh over the cheese layer.
13) Invert the knafeh on a ghee-greased serving platter so that the cheese layer is on the bottom and the crust is on top. The knafeh should have about 3/4 cup of cooled scented sugar syrup on its surface. Using a spatula, spread the syrup out to even out the saturation. If desired, sprinkle the surface with ground pistachios. Cut into squares and serve immediately while still warm and the cheddar is as yet gooey. Dollop with fresh eshta and, if desired, drizzle with additional syrup. Reheat the knafeh by placing the serving platter over a simmering water bath if serving later. The cheese will remelt and remain gooey for a long time thanks to the steam from the hot water. Knafeh tastes best the day it is made.

### KATAIFI: SHREDDED PHYLLO WITH NUTS & HONEY SYRUP

Prep time : 10 minutes

Cook Time: 45 minutes

Servings: 2-3 servings

## INGREDIENTS

- 1 package kataifi dough (1 pound), completely thawed out and at room temperature.
- 1 pound unsalted butter, melted

**Filling:**

- 1 cup ground walnuts
- 1 cup ground almonds
- 1/4 cup sugar
- 1/4 cup panko breadcrumbs
- 1/4 cup orange juice or lemon juice
- 1 teaspoon ground cinnamon
- 1/2 teaspoon ground cloves

**Syrup:**

- 2 cups honey

- 1 cup sugar
- 2 and 1/2 cups water
- 1-2 cinnamon sticks
- orange peel or lemon peel
- 1/4 cup orange juice or lemon juice

## INSTRUCTIONS

1) Bake at 350 degrees Fahrenheit.
2) Make the syrup first. In a saucepan, combine all of the ingredients for the syrup and bring to a boil. Decrease intensity to medium and cook until the sugar breaks up. Allow to completely cool.
3) In a bowl, thoroughly combine all of the filling ingredients.
4) Keep in mind to let the kataifi dough come to room temperature after it has been defrosted.
5) Make the butter melt.
6) Separate the kataifi batter into around 18 equivalent segments. To prevent them from becoming dry, cover them with a dry, clean towel and then cover that with a damp towel.
7) Brush each section with melted butter one at a time. Place a spoonful of the filling on the dough strip's bottom. To prevent the filling from spilling out, roll upward, paying attention to the sides.
8) Place in a 9x13 inch baking plate. The procedure should be repeated until all of the rolled-out kataifi dough strips have been filled.
9) Pour the excess margarine over the cakes.
10) Bake until golden, about 45 minutes.
11) The cooled, strained syrup should all be poured over the kataifi. Serve after the pastry has had time to absorb the syrup. Never cover the hot pastry with hot syrup. Put hot syrup on top of cooled pastry or put cool syrup on top of hot pastry.
12) Any remaining filling can be stored in the freezer in a Ziploc bag for later use.

# ATAYEF

Prep Time : 30 minutes

Cook Time: 10 minutes

Servings: 8 servings

## INGREDIENTS

- 1½ cups all-purpose flour
- 2 tsp. baking powder
- 2 tb. white granulated sugar
- 1½ cups water Room Temp.
- 2 cups whole milk ricotta cheese
- ¼ cup crushed pistachios
- Rose water simple syrup (attar) For serving

### Rose Water Syrup

- 2 cups granulated sugar
- 1 cup water
- 1 tb. lemon juice
- 1 tsp. orange blossom water
- 2 tsp. rose water

## INSTRUCTIONS

1) Combine all of the dry ingredients (flour, sugar, and baking powder) in a large bowl.
2) Add the water to the consolidated dry fixings and blend well. The consistency of the mixture ought to be similar to that of a batter for pancakes that is runnier. Put away to rest for 15 minutes.
3) Heat up a non-stick skillet on medium-low intensity. Use the bottom of a spoon or ladle to lightly spread a tablespoon or two of batter.
4) The bubbles in the Atayef will begin. When there are not any more sparkly (crude player) regions, eliminate the hotcake utilizing a spatula and put on a light kitchen towel or paper towels. This will require 1-2 minutes.
5) The Atayef's bottom ought to be a light brown color.
6) In a bowl, mix the ricotta cheese to make the filling. To give the filling a wonderful rose water flavor, stir in one tablespoon of the rose-water simple syrup.
7) Place about 1 tablespoon of filling on each Atayef pancake once they have completely cooled.
8) To close it halfway, pinch the sides together.
9) Plunge the open part of the stuffed Atayef into the squashed pistachios.
10) Serve plain or with simple syrup.

# SAHLAB (MIDDLE EASTERN MILK PUDDING)

Prep Time: 5 minutes

Cook Time: 10 minutes

Servings: 4 servings

## INGREDIENTS

- 4 cups (1 litre) whole milk
- 3 ½ tablespoons (25 g) cornstarch cornflour in the UK
- 6 teaspoons granulated sugar
- 1 teaspoon pure vanilla extract
- ½ teaspoon ground cinnamon
- 1 tablespoon (20 g) desiccated coconut
- ¼ cup chopped nuts walnuts or pistachios
- 2 tablespoons raisins optional

## INSTRUCTIONS

1) Beat the milk, cornstarch, sugar, and vanilla extract with a whisk over medium heat.
2) Bring the mixture to a boil and stir frequently for two minutes. or until it's thick and creamy.
3) Pour into mugs and top each serving with cinnamon, desiccated coconut, pistachios, or walnuts.

# GHRAYBEH MIDDLE EASTERN BUTTER COOKIE

Prep Time : 10 minutes

Cook Time: 12 minutes

Servings: 4 serving

## INGREDIENTS

- 2 cups all-purpose flour
- 1 ¼ confectioner's sugar powdered sugar
- 1 cup cold ghee
- ½ teaspoon vanilla optional
- Pistachios to garnish the cookies

## INSTRUCTIONS

1) Beat the ghee with a hand mixer or a stand mixer until it is light in color and has a fluffy texture.
2) Continue beating the ghee with the confectioner's sugar until it resembles buttercream.
3) Beat for a few seconds before adding the vanilla.
4) Decrease the blender's speed and add the flour. Use a spatula or wooden spoon to mix for a few seconds, then use a stand mixer to mix until the ingredients are well combined.
5) Refrigerate the dough for 20 to 30 minutes by wrapping it in plastic.
6) Use parchment paper to line a baking sheet.
7) Form balls of equal size and place them over the previously prepared baking sheet. The balls should weigh 15 to 16 grams.
8) You can either leave the balls as they are or place one pistachio on top of each ball and gently press the pistachio into the cookie's center.
9) The ghraybeh cookies that have been formed should be refrigerated for twenty minutes.
10) Bake the cookies in the middle rack of the oven for 10 to 12 minutes at 160 C/325 F.
11) Remove the cookies from the oven and allow them to cool on the baking sheet for a few minutes. While the cookies are still warm, do not move them from the baking sheet or touch them.
12) Set the cookies on a rack to cool. Forget about the treats and revealed for essentially an hour to ensure it's not warm since, supposing that you place the treats in a holder while warm, the dampness will make the treats hard.
13) Store the treats in a holder and leave at room temperature for as long as seven days.

# MAAMOUL (ARABIAN DATE FILLED COOKIES)

Prep Time : 1 hour

Cook Time: 25 minutes

Servings: 10 serving

## INGREDIENTS

### For The Dough

- ¼ c milk
- ¼ tsp active dry yeast
- 2 c unbleached all-purpose flour
- 1 Tbsp sugar
- 2 Tbsp canola oil
- 6 Tbsp clarified butter or unsalted butter, melted
- ½ tsp pure vanilla extract
- ¼ c water

### For the Filling

- 4 oz dried dates, pitted and chopped
- 1 ½ tsp canola oil
- 1/8 tsp pure almond extract
- ¼ tsp cinnamon
- 1/8 tsp ground cardamom
- Pinch anise
- 1 Tbsp water

### For Dusting

- ¼ c powdered sugar

## INSTRUCTIONS

1) Mix the milk and yeast together in a small bowl. Set aside for 3-5 minutes or until the yeast has softened and formed a foam.
2) Mix the sugar and flour in a medium bowl.
3) With your fingertips, work the melted butter and oil into the flour until it has an even, sandy texture.
4) Add the yeast and milk blend and vanilla. Utilizing your fingers, mix gently.
5) Mix gently after each addition of water until the dough comes together to form a soft, shaggy dough.
6) Cover the batter and put away to rest for 10 minutes, while you set up the filling.
7) In a small saucepan, combine the filling ingredients with the chopped dates.

8) Cover the saucepan and heat, stirring occasionally, for 7 to 10 minutes, until the dates become soft and the consistency of jam.
9) Preheat your stove to 350F.
10) Separate the batter into 1 Tbsp segments. Form a ball from each section.
11) Level one bundle of batter into a plate and put 1 tsp of filling on the middle. To seal in the filling, fold the dough's edges around it and press them together.
12) To return the filled cookie to its original ball shape, gently roll it between your hands. After that, slightly flatten the cookie.
13) Enhance, whenever wanted, utilizing a fork or press the filled treat into a floured form and tap it out.
14) Place the filled and shaped cookies one inch apart on a baking sheet lined with parchment.
15) The baking sheet should be rotated once during the time the cookies are baking for 25 minutes. When the cookies are lightly golden brown, take them out.
16) Before dusting the maamoul with powdered sugar, allow it to completely cool.
17) Store the maamoul in an impenetrable holder on the counter for 2-3 weeks.

## KAHK, (EID COOKIES) WITH PISTACHIOS AND HONEY

Prep Time : 1 hour

Cook Time: 30 minutes

Servings: 20 cookies

### INGREDIENTS

- 3 cups flour.
- a dash of salt - approximately ⅛ teaspoon.
- 1 Tablespoon granulated sugar.
- ½ teaspoon cinnamon.
- 3 Tablespoons toasted sesame seeds- optional but highly recommended.
- ½ teaspoon dry yeast.
- 1 cup ghee- room temperature and not melted.
- ⅓ cup warm water

### For the pistachios and honey filling

- 1 Tablespoon ghee or butter.
- 1 Tablespoon flour.
- 1 teaspoon sesame seeds.
- ¼ cup honey.
- ½ cup pistachios coarsely ground.

**For garnishing**

- Powdered sugar.

## INSTRUCTIONS

1) Add the flour, cinnamon, sesame seeds, sugar, yeast, and salt to your mixing bowl.
2) Mix in the melted, room-temperature ghee until completely incorporated.
3) Add water and keep blending until you get a decent steady batter.
4) Cover it and give it an hour to rest.
5) Let's make the filling in the meantime. Flour should be mixed with ghee or butter in a small pot over medium heat until it turns golden brown.
6) After removing the pan from the heat, thoroughly combine the honey and sesame seeds before returning the mixture to a low heat to thicken.
7) Mix in the pistachios after removing the pan from the heat. Allow it to chill off for 10 minutes then structure into 20 little balls.
8) Divide the dough equally into 20 balls of about 40 grams each after an hour has passed.
9) Cover a plate with plastic wrap and place the dough balls there.
10) The kahk will now be filled and shaped.
11) Take a ball of dough, place one ball of the pistachio filling in the middle, and then roll the dough into a ball.
12) Press softly into a Mamoul instrument or you can simply make some etching utilizing a fork.
13) Bake the cookies for 20 to 25 minutes, or until the bottoms are golden brown, on a cookie sheet lined with parchment paper at 350 degrees Fahrenheit.
14) Allow it to chill off on a wire rack. Make sure the container is airtight.
15) Sprinkle the top with powdered sugar when you're ready to enjoy.

# LGEIMAT: SAFFRON AND CARDAMOM FRITTERS

Prep Time : 20 minutes

Cook Time: 10 minutes

Servings: 20 serving

## INGREDIENTS

**For the Syrup:**

- 1 cup sugar
- 1/2 cup water
- 1 tablespoon lemon juice
- 1/2 teaspoon cardamom
- 1/2 teaspoon cinnamon
- 1 teaspoon saffron
- Pinch of salt

**For the Fritters:**

- 2 cups all purpose flour
- 1 tablespoon baking powder
- 1 teaspoon baking soda
- 1 teaspoon salt
- 1 tablespoon sugar
- 1 cup full-fat yogurt (Greek-style)
- 1 egg
- 4 cups canola oil (or enough to measure a depth of 2 inches, for frying)
- Garnish: strips of lemon rind

## INSTRUCTIONS

1) Collect the supplies.
2) In a large pot, combine the sugar, water, lemon juice, cinnamon, saffron, and a pinch of salt to make the syrup. Stir as it simmers until the sugar is dissolved. Permit to sit while you make the wastes.
3) Sift the all-purpose flour, sugar, baking soda, and baking powder into a large bowl.
4) Whisk the egg and Greek yogurt together in a separate bowl.
5) Mix the dry ingredients with the wet until a dough forms. Give yourself about ten minutes to rest.
6) In an enormous pot, heat the oil to 350 F.
7) Utilizing a tablespoon or treat scoop (somewhere in the range of 1/2-to 1-ounce relying upon what you have), scoop the mixture into the hot oil. Work in groups so as not to stuff the pot.

8) The fritters should be browned on all sides by being stirred around. Each batch should be fried for two to three minutes total. Drain them on a paper towel when they have turned brown.
9) Move each one to a bowl after it has been fried, then top it with lemon rind strips or zest and the syrup. Serve right away.

## BASBOUSA: ALMOND COCONUT SEMOLINA CAKE RECIPE

Prep Time : 15 minutes

Cook Time: 45 minutes

Servings: 8 serving

## INGREDIENTS

- ½ cup plus 2 tablespoon unsalted butter
- 1 cup sugar
- 1 cup plain yogurt
- 1 cup fine semolina PLUS 1 cup coarse semolina (or 2 cups coarse semolina or 2 cups original Cream of Wheat enriched farina)
- ⅓ cup milk
- 1 tsp baking powder
- ¼ cup sweetened shredded coconut or coconut chips
- ¼ cup shaved almonds

**Cinnamon Simple Syrup:**

- 1 ½ cup sugar
- 1 ¾ cup water
- 1 short cinnamon stick
- ¼ tsp lemon juice

## INSTRUCTIONS

1) Preheat the broiler to 350 degrees F.
2) Place the margarine in a little bowl and dissolve in the microwave. Place aside.
3) Sugar and yogurt should be combined in a large mixing bowl. Now incorporate the milk, baking powder, and semolina. At last mix in the dissolved spread, and let the blend sit momentarily so the margarine is assimilated.
4) Place the semolina mixture in a 9-inch round cake pan or baking dish that has been lightly greased. For about 40 to 45 minutes, bake in an oven heated to 350 degrees Fahrenheit. Broil the basbousa for a brief time if necessary to color the top. Take careful note. Remove from the oven when ready.

5) Make the cinnamon simple syrup while the cake is baking. Sugar, water, and the cinnamon stick should be combined in a small saucepan or sauce pan. Stir as it comes to a boil over high heat until the sugar is dissolved. Cook for a few minutes on low heat until the syrup thickens. Add the lemon juice after taking the pan off the heat. After it has completely cooled, take the cinnamon stick out.
6) Pour the chilled syrup over the hot basbousa as soon as it comes out of the oven. Let cool totally; syrup should be consumed into the cake. Before serving, allow it to sit for one hour for best results.
7) Top the cake with the coconut chips, coconut, and shaved almonds when it's ready to serve. Enjoy the slice!

## EGYPTIAN KOSHARI RECIPE

Cook Time: 1 hour 22 minutes

Servings: 4-6 serving

## INGREDIENTS

### For the Crispy Onion Topping
- 1 large onion, sliced into thin rings
- Salt
- ⅓ cup all-purpose flour
- ½ cup cooking oil

### For Tomato Sauce
- Cooking oil
- 1 small onion, grated
- 4 garlic cloves, minced
- 1 tsp ground coriander
- ½ -1 teaspoon crushed red pepper flakes (optional)
- 1 can 28-oz tomato sauce
- Salt and pepper
- 1-2 tablespoon distilled white vinegar

### For Koshari
- 1 ½ cup brown lentils, picked over and well-rinsed
- 1 ½ cup medium-grain rice, rinsed, soaked in water for 15 minutes, drained
- ½ tsp each salt and pepper
- ½ tsp coriander
- 2 cups elbow pasta
- Cooking oil

- Water
- 1 15-oz can chickpeas, rinsed, drained and warmed

## INSTRUCTIONS

1) Sprinkle the onion rings with salt, then toss them in the flour to coat. Shake off excess flour.
2) In a large skillet, heat the cooking oil over medium-high heat, cook the onion rings, stirring often, until they turn a nice caramelized brown. Onions must be crispy, but not burned (15-20 minutes).
3) In a saucepan, heat 1 tablespoon cooking oil. Add the grated onion, cook on medium-high until the onion turns a translucent gold (do not brown). Now add the garlic, coriander, and red pepper flakes, if using, and saute briefly until fragrant (30-45 seconds more).
4) Stir in tomato sauce and pinch of salt. Bring to a simmer and cook until the sauce thickens (15 minutes or so).
5) Stir in the distilled white vinegar, and turn the heat to low. Cover and keep warm until ready to serve.
6) Cook the lentils. Bring lentils and 4 cups of water to a boil in a medium pot or saucepan over high heat. Reduce the heat to low and cook until lentils are just tender (15-17 minutes). Drain from water and season with a little salt. (Note: when the lentils are ready, they should not be fully cooked. They should be only par-cooked and still have a bite to them as they need to finish cooking with the rice).
7) Now, for the rice. Drain the rice from its soaking water. Combine the par-cooked lentils and the rice in the saucepan over medium-high heat with 1 tablespoon cooking oil, salt, pepper, and coriander. Cook for 3 minutes, stirring regularly. Add warm water to cover the rice and lentil mixture by about 1 ½ inches (you'll probably use about 3 cups of water here). Bring to a boil; the water should reduce a bit. Now cover and cook until all the liquid has been absorbed and both the rice and lentils are well cooked through (about 20 minutes). Keep covered and undisturbed for 5 minutes or so.
8) Now make the pasta. While the rice and lentils are cooking, make the pasta according to package instructions by adding the elbow pasta to boiling water with a dash of salt and a little oil. Cook until the pasta is al dente. Drain.
9) Cover the chickpeas and warm in the microwave briefly before serving.

# SPICY LENTIL SOUP

Prep Time : 15 minutes

Cook Time: 50 minutes

Servings: 6-8 serving

## INGREDIENTS

- 2 tablespoons extra-virgin olive oil
- 1 medium yellow onion, diced
- 1 large celery rib, diced
- 1 large carrot, diced
- 4 large garlic cloves, minced
- 1 large baking potato, peeled and chopped into 1/2" pieces
- 1.5 cups red lentils
- 2 quarts vegetable broth
- 2 teaspoon ground cumin
- 1 teaspoon smoked paprika
- 1/2 teaspoon ancho chili powder
- 1/2 teaspoon ground black pepper
- 1/4 teaspoon cayenne pepper (add more or less, depending on your heat preference)
- 1/4 teaspoon turmeric
- 2 tablespoon freshly squeezed lemon juice, plus additional lemon slices for squeezing over the top of finished soup
- kosher salt, as needed
- plain Greek yogurt, optional garnish
- chopped cilantro, optional garnish

## INSTRUCTIONS

1) Place a small stockpot or large saucepan on medium-high heat. Add the oil once it is hot. Add the onion, celery, and carrot to the oil and stir until they begin to shimmer. Cook for 8 minutes, mixing sporadically. Cook for an additional two minutes, stirring frequently, before adding the garlic. Include the lentils, potato, and vegetable broth. Turn up intensity to medium-high and heat to the point of boiling. After that, reduce the heat to medium-low and stir in the turmeric, cumin, ancho chili powder, black pepper, and cayenne pepper. Cover and simmer for 40 to 50 minutes, or until all the vegetables are very tender.
2) Using an immersion blender, carefully puree the soup in the pot until the vegetables are completely smooth. Or, in smaller batches, carefully transfer hot soup to a blender, blend it until smooth, and then return the soup to the pot. Add the juice of a lemon. Taste the dish and add salt if necessary.

3) Ladle hot soup into individual bowls and top with freshly squeezed lemon wedges for serving. Warm pitas or flatbread for dipping and plain Greek yogurt with chopped cilantro, if desired, are additional flavors.

# FATTAH

Prep Time : 30 minutes

Cook Time: 3hours

Servings: 6-8 serving

## INGREDIENTS

**For the meat:**
- 1 Tablespoon ghee/unsalted butter.
- 2-3 mastic pieces.
- 2 pounds beef/lamb cut into 2-inch squares. See notes below for best cuts.
- 2 bay leaves.
- ¼ teaspoon ground cardamom.
- ¼ teaspoon sugar.
- ½ teaspoon black pepper.
- 1 medium onion quartered.
- 1(100g) Roma tomato quartered.
- 2 (70g )celery stalks, cubes almost half a cup.
- 1 garlic clove.
- 1 large (60g) carrot cut into chunks.
- Boiling water to cover.
- 1 teaspoon salt I've used pink salt.

**For the rice:**
- 1 Tablespoon ghee or unsalted butter.
- 1 Tablespoon olive oil.
- 2 cups (400g) short grain or jasmine rice.
- 2 ¼ cup hot water/beef broth or a mixture.
- Salt to taste.

**For the sauces:**
- 1 Tablespoon ghee/unsalted butter.
- 1 Tablespoon olive oil.
- 5 large garlic cloves minced.
- ¼ cup white vinegar.
- 2 cups tomato sauce.
- 2 Tablespoons tomato paste.

- 1 teaspoon 7-spice blend.
- Salt and pepper to taste.
- 3 cups beef/lamb broth divided.
- 6 Pita bread loaves. more or less depending on your liking. cut into 1 inch squares.

## INSTRUCTIONS

1. In a profound pot liquefy margarine or ghee over medium high intensity, add mastic and mix until mastic pieces are liquefied.
2. Brown all over after adding meat cubes.
3. Stir in the cardamom, sugar, bay leaves, and black pepper.
4. Include the carrots, celery, onion, garlic, and tomato. Combine everything thoroughly.
5. Pour in hot bubbling water to cover. Eliminate any froth ascending at the surface.
6. Reduce the heat and bring the pot to a boil. Put a loose lid on the pot and let it simmer until it's done.
7. Put away to chill off a little, eliminate vegetables and cove leaves with an opened spoon. Season the vegetables and eat them or throw them out if you want to.
8. Cover and set aside the beef cubes on a plate.
9. Set aside the broth as well after straining it through a sieve.
10. Add butter and oil to a medium-sized pot.
11. Add the rice after the butter has melted.
12. For two to three minutes, stir the rice until it is completely coated in the butter and oil mixture.
13. Season with salt, add water or broth, and bring to a boil.
14. Lessen intensity, cover and let it cook for 13-15 minutes.
15. Slice the bread into 1-inch squares and preheat the oven to 350°F. Place everything on a baking sheet.
16. The baking sheet should be in the middle of your oven.
17. Bake for 10 to 12 minutes, or until the bottoms and edges are golden brown and crisp.
18. Set aside after removing from the oven.
19. Olive oil and butter should be melted in a saucepan on medium heat.
20. Stir in the garlic and cook for 30 to 1 minute, or until it is lightly browned and fragrant.
21. After adding the vinegar, cook the mixture for three to four minutes. Heat up less.
22. Set aside about half of the garlic in a small bowl.
23. Mix in the tomato sauce, 7-spice blend, salt, and pepper after increasing the heat to medium again.
24. Add the tomato glue and pour in one cup of the stock you have.
25. To thicken, bring to a boil, then reduce the heat and simmer for ten minutes.
26. Pour the remaining broth into another saucepan and bring to a boil.
27. Scoop out the garlic-vinegar mixture and add it.
28. After adding salt and pepper, turn off the heat.
29. Put the toasted pita on the platter then shower with around 1 cup of the white sauce.
    Note 3: After leveling the rice, arrange the meat on top of or around the platter.

30. Top with some tomato sauce.
31. Serve the bowls with the remaining tomato sauce and white sauce on the side.

# **FUL BURIED**

Cook Time: 35 minutes

Servings: 6 servings

## INGREDIENTS

- 2 cups small Egyptian fava beans (ful buried), soaked overnight (and left unpeeled)
- Salt
- 1/3 cup chopped flat-leaf parsley
- Extra-virgin olive oil
- 3 lemons, quartered
- Salt and pepper
- 4–6 cloves garlic, crushed
- Chili-pepper flakes
- Cumin

## INSTRUCTIONS

1) As the cooking time fluctuates relying upon the quality and age of the beans, it is great to cook them ahead of time and to warm them when you are prepared to serve. In a large saucepan with a lid, cook the drained beans in a fresh portion of unsalted water until tender. When the beans are soft, add salt and cover with water. They need two to two and a half hours of gentle simmering. At the point when the beans are delicate, let the fluid diminish. Typically, a few ladles of beans are removed and mashed with some of the cooking liquid before being stirred back into the beans. This is to make the sauce thicker.
2) Arab bread should be served alongside the beans in soup bowls and sprinkled with chopped parsley.
3) Distribute the ingredients for the dressing so that everyone can serve themselves: a jug of extra-virgin olive oil, the quartered lemons, salt and pepper, a little saucer with the squashed garlic, one with stew pepper chips, and one with ground cumin.
4) The beans are eaten delicately squashed with the fork, so they retain the dressing.
5) One hard-boiled egg per person should be peeled and chopped for the beans in the bowl.
6) A salad of cucumber, tomato, and thinly sliced mild onions or scallions serve as toppings for the beans. In any case, distribute a large quantity of scallions, quartered tomatoes, and cucumber sticks.

7) Present with tahina cream sauce or salad, with pickles and cut onions absorbed vinegar for 30 minutes.
8) One more approach to serving ful buried is covered in a garlicky pureed tomatoes.
9) They consume full buried with olives, small cucumbers, yogurt, or feta cheese in Syria and Lebanon.
10) A conventional approach to thickening the sauce is to toss a small bunch of red lentils (1/4 cup) into the water toward the beginning of the cooking.
11) In the Iraqi dish known as badkila, which is also sold for breakfast on the street, large brown beans are used in place of the smaller Egyptian varieties.

## HOMEMADE EGYPTIAN HAWAWSHI

Prep Time : 15 minutes

Cook Time: 15 minutes

Servings: 12 servings

## INGREDIENTS

- 1 large yellow onion quartered
- 2 garlic cloves
- 1 green bell pepper cored and cut into large chunks
- 1 jalapeno halved and seeded (leave some of the seed if you like heat)
- ½ ounce fresh parsley stems trimmed (cut most of the stem but leave some for extra flavor)
- 2 lbs lean ground beef
- 3 tablespoon tomato paste
- Kosher salt
- Extra virgin olive oil
- 6 loaves of pita bread you need the kind with pockets

**For The Hawawshi Seasoning (Spice Mixture)**

- 1 teaspoon coriander
- 1 teaspoon allspice
- 1 teaspoon paprika
- 1 teaspoon black pepper
- ½ teaspoon cumin
- ¾ teaspoon cardamom
- ¼ teaspoon cinnamon

## INSTRUCTIONS

1) Make sure the oven is at 400 degrees Fahrenheit. Combine the spices in a small bowl.
2) In a bowl of a food processor with a blade, pulse the onion, garlic, bell pepper, jalapeno, and parsley until finely chopped. Use the back of a spoon to push the mixture through a sieve to remove any excess liquid.
3) The onion mixture should go into a large mixing bowl. Add the ground meat and tomato glue. Combine by mixing. Kosher salt and the spice mixture should be added. Blend again until the combination is very much consolidated and the flavors are all around dispersed inside the meat combination.
4) 12 pita pockets can be made by slicing the pita bread in half.
5) Set up a huge sheet skillet brushed with a touch of additional virgin olive oil.
6) Fill one-third of a cup of the meat mixture into each pita pocket. Spread the meat mixture inside the pita pockets with the back of a spoon.
7) Organize the pitas in the pre-arranged sheet container. A little extra virgin olive oil can be used to brush the tops of the pita pockets.
8) Prepare in the warmed broiler for 15, then, at that point, cautiously turn the pitas over and cook on the opposite side one more 5 to 10 minutes until the meat is completely cooked and the pita is fresh on the two sides.

# SLOW COOKER EGYPTIAN LENTILS AND RIC

Prep Time : 10 minutes

Cook Time: 4 minutes

Servings: 8 servings

## INGREDIENTS

- 1 cup green lentils use red lentils if you want it to cook quicker
- ¾ teaspoon salt
- 4 ½ teaspoons olive oil
- 1 large onion chopped
- ¾ teaspoon cinnamon
- 1 ¼ tablespoon ground cumin
- ¼ teaspoon pepper
- ½ cup jasmine rice or brown or white rice
- 6 cups vegetable stock or water or chicken stock

## INSTRUCTIONS

1) Place the olive oil into the lower part of the sluggish cooker.
2) Include the stock among the remaining ingredients.
3) Cover and cook for 6-7 hours on low or 3-4 hours on high.
4) Mix the combination while it is in the sluggish cooker. On the off chance that it is dry, add a little water In the event that it's soup-like, eliminate top for a brief period, or go intensity to high setting.
5) If you use red lentils, cook them for about two hours. Keep an eye on the time.
6) Present with slashed green onions, new cilantro, or hacked red onions.

# EGYPTIAN TOMATO SAUCE

Prep Time : 5 minutes

Cook Time: 40 minutes

Servings: 4-6 servings

## INGREDIENTS

- 1 onion, finely chopped
- 5 -7 garlic, crushed
- 2 cups tomato juice
- 1 teaspoon vinegar
- 2 tablespoons oil (can add more)
- salt and pepper
- 1 teaspoon sugar

## INSTRUCTIONS

- Saute onions med heat until quite brown.
- add garlic and cook only a little.
- add tomato juice and sugar and cook 15-20mins.
- Add vinegar and seasoning and cook 2 -3 minutes.

# SRIRACHA DEVILED EGGS WITH SPICY BREAD CRUMBS

Prep Time : 30 minutes

Cook Time: 40 minutes

Servings: 6 servings

## INGREDIENTS

**For the rice mixture:**

- 3 Tablespoons olive oil.
- 1 medium yellow onion Chopped.
- 2 Tablespoons tomato paste.
- 1 can (16oz) tomato sauce.
- 2 cups short grain rice Note1.
- 1 cup fresh parsley chopped. Note2
- ½ cup fresh cilantro chopped. Note2
- ⅓ cup fresh dill chopped. Note2
- 1 Tablespoon dry mint.

- ½ teaspoon ground black pepper.
- ½ teaspoon salt or to taste.

**The above mixture is enough for one of the following: Note3**
- 4 pounds Mexican squash.
- 2.8 or almost 3 pounds Anaheim pepper.
- 2.8 or almost 3 pounds white or Japanese eggplant.
- ½ pound grape leaves.

**Cooking liquid:**
- 2 ½ cup hot stock or water.
- 1 bouillon cube.
- 1 teaspoon tomato paste.

## INSTRUCTIONS

1) Add oil to a pot with a medium heat and sauté the onions for two to three minutes until translucent.
2) Include the paste and tomato sauce. To dissolve the tomato paste, stir.
3) Add the rice, herbs, and spices when it starts to bubble, and cook for just two minutes.
4) Remove from heat and set aside to cool.
5) Note4: Wash the vegetables thoroughly and thoroughly.
6) When chopping vegetables, especially zucchini and eggplant, be careful not to tear the walls.
7) I usually like to cut Anaheim pepper in half for easy stuffing, and I always buy long, straight ones.
8) Fill each one with the rice mixture, making sure not to fill them all the way to the top. You should leave about 12 centimeters of space at the top of the vegetable.
9) Rice will extend subsequent to cooking and assuming you are overstuffing the veggies, rice will fall off. It won't taste bad, but the way it's presented won't be as fancy.
10) To prevent scorching, arrange the stems of herbs, the inside of the vegetables you just removed, lemon slices, tomato slices, or onion slices at the bottom of your cooking pot.
11) Put the stuffed vegetables in the pot.
12) In the hot water, dissolve the tomato paste and bouillon.
13) Fill the pot so the cooking fluid is part of the way through the veggies layers.
14) Put pot on medium high, heat to the point of boiling then, at that point, diminish intensity and stew for 40 minutes until veggies are cooked. Note 6: Before serving, allow it to slightly cool down.

# CHICKEN SHAWARMA

Prep Time : 10 minutes

Cook Time: 1 hour

Servings: 4-6 servings

## INGREDIENTS

- 1 pound boneless skinless chicken breasts (2 large breasts)
- 1 pound boneless skinless chicken thighs (4 large thighs)
- 6 tablespoons extra virgin olive oil divided
- 2 teaspoons cumin
- 2 teaspoons paprika
- 1 teaspoon allspice
- 3/4 teaspoon turmeric
- 1/4 teaspoon garlic powder
- 1/4 teaspoon cinnamon
- 1 pinch cayenne
- Salt and black pepper
- Nonstick cooking oil spray

## INSTRUCTIONS

1) For convenience, just mix the marinade directly in a ziplock bag. A bag works best because the chicken remains nicely coated in the marinade. If you prefer to use a container, either turn the chicken a few times or increase the marinade by 50%.
2) Add chicken into the marinade. Seal the bag, removing excess air, then massage to coat from the outside. Leave to marinade for 12 to 24 hours in the fridge. If you're pressed for time, even 3 hours will do!
3) Yogurt sauce – Make the yogurt sauce simply by mixing the ingredients then set aside for at least 20 minutes to let the flavours meld. This will keep for 3 days in the fridge.
4) Cook chicken either on the stove or on the BBQ. It will get a great crust on it from the spices, and you will adore the smell. It's intoxicating!
5) Rest chicken for at least 3 minutes before serving to allow the juices to redistribute throughout the flesh, else they will just run out everywhere when you slice the meat.
6) To serve, just pile everything on a platter and let everybody make their own wraps! The chicken, lettuce, tomato slices, onion, yogurt sauce and warmed flatbreads – homemade or store bought. If the chicken is on the larger side, I sometimes slice it. But if they are smaller, I tend to just leave them whole.

# EGYPTIAN MAHLAB BREAD

Prep Time: 10 minutes

Cook Time: 2-3 minutes

Servings: 2-3 breads

## INGREDIENTS

- 3 cup flour.
- ½ teaspoon salt.
- 1 ½ teaspoon dry yeast.
- ½ teaspoon sugar - optional didn't use.
- 1 cup warm water
- 1 egg mixed with 1 tablespoon milk

## INSTRUCTIONS

1) In your mixing bowl, mix flour, salt , yeast and sugar if using, until well combined.
2) Slowly add water until it forms a soft and smooth dough.
3) Place in an oiled bowl and let it rise for an hour or until doubled in size.
4) Divide the dough into 16 equal parts - more or less according to the size of the bread you need.
5) Flatten the balls to a 2mm thickness, brush top with egg and milk mixture and sprinkle black seeds on top.
6) Let it rest for another 10-15 minutes, meanwhile pre-heat your oven to 400F.
7) Place the bread into the oven and bake for 15 to 20 minutes until the bottom is lightly brown.
8) If the top of the bread is not golden brown yet, you may want to open the broiler on low for about 2 to 3 minutes and watching carefully.
9) Take the bread out and let it cool completely to room temperature.
10) Bread will harden as it cools down.

# SALATA BALADI

Prep Time : 15 minutes

Servings: 3 servings

## INGREDIENTS

- 3 firm Roma tomatoes , diced
- 2 mini cucumbers , diced
- 3 tablespoons finely chopped fresh parsley
- 1 bell pepper , diced
- 1 small red onion , peeled and diced
- 1 lemon (freshly squeezed)
- 1 tablespoon white vinegar
- ½ teaspoon fleur de sel
- ¼ teaspoon ground cumin
- ¼ teaspoon red pepper
- 2 tablespoons olive oil

## INSTRUCTIONS

1) In a bowl, mix all the ingredients.
2) Serve fresh.

# EGYPTIAN GARLIC YOGURT CUCUMBER SALAD

Prep Time: 7 minutes

Servings: 4-5 servings

## INGREDIENTS

- 4 ounces plain yogurt (you could use a 6 oz container too, no problem)
- 1/2 cucumber (grated fine)
- 3 garlic cloves (crushed)
- 1 tablespoon white vinegar
- 1 teaspoon fresh dill (chopped- you could use dry dill, but fresh better)
- salt & pepper

## INSTRUCTION

1) Fill a small mixing bowl with yogurt.
2) In the yogurt, grate the half cucumber.
3) Press the garlic into the bowl with a garlic press.
4) Salt and pepper to taste, chopped dill, and vinegar.
5) Best after being chilled for about 30 minutes.
6) Keeps well for a few days in the refrigerator.
7) Warm pita bread is a good dipping option.

# TOUM RECIPE FOR THE WORLD'S STRONGEST LEBANESE GARLIC SAUCE

Prep Time: 10 minutes

Servings: 20 servings

## INGREDIENTS

- 3 Heads garlic pealed
- 4 cups vegetable oil Avocado/canola/sunflower/peanut etc...
- 1/2 cup lemon juice fresh
- 1 teaspoon salt or to taste

## INSTRUCTIONS

1. Ensure that all ingredients are at room temperature for a more reliable outcome. Also if you are using a large food processor make sure you use at least 3 heads of garlic otherwise smaller quantities of garlic won't be easily reached by large blades.
2. Add the garlic and salt in the food processor and run for 10-20 seconds.
3. Stop processor, scrap garlic down the sides, then run processor again for another 10-20 seconds. Repeat process 3-4 times until garlic starts to turn pasty.
4. From this point onwards, turn the processor back on and keep it on until the end.
5. Start adding the oil slowly in a very thin stream. After adding the first half cup you will start seeing the garlic emulsify and turn into a shiny paste already.
6. While still running, add ½ teaspoon of lemon juice very slowly, in a thin stream.
7. Wait on it a few seconds until the lemon juice is well absorbed then go back to repeating the same process of slowly adding ½ cup of oil in a thin stream, waiting a few seconds, then adding ½ teaspoon of lemon juice until you've used all ingredients. This process should take 8-10 minutes.

# BEST EVER OM ALI (EGYPTIAN BREAD PUDDING)

Prep Time: 15 minutes

Cook Time: 5 minutes

Servings: 4-6 servings

## INGREDIENTS

- 500 g/1lb palmiers (also known as lunettes), storebought or homemade*
- 1 liter/1 quart (4 1/4 cups) full fat milk, preferably organic buffalo*
- 1/2 cup (100g) granulated sugar
- 250g/8oz (1 cup) fresh eshta balady (country-style clotted cream) or 1 cup heavy whipping cream, (whipped to medium peaks)
- OPTIONAL ASSORTED NUTS OF YOUR CHOICE (TO SERVE ON THE SIDE OR TO INCORPORATE INTO THE DESSERT) L USED:
- 1/2 cup (57g) toasted hazelnuts, coarsely chopped
- 1/2 cup (57g) pistachios, coarsely chopped
- 1/2 cup (75g) raisins
- 1/4 cup (20g) shredded coconut

## INSTRUCTIONS

1) Set the oven rack to the medium position and preheat the broiler to 200C/390F. Divide the palmiers in half and layer them in an oven-safe baking dish. The remaining 1/4 of the palmiers should be put aside. If you're using nuts, add them. Because not everyone likes nuts, I prefer to serve it on the side.
2) Mix the milk and sugar in a medium saucepan over medium heat until the sugar dissolves, then bring to a boil.
3) Over the palmiers, spread the boiling milk mixture.
4) Utilize the saved 1/4 measure of palmers to top the outer layer of the milk-drenched palmiers. The result will be a topping that is even crunchier.
5) Eshta spoons should be used to dot the surface of the dish. There's no need to share it. Spread the whipped cream over the dish in an even layer to cover the entire surface.
6) Broil the dish under the broiler in the oven until golden brown on top and bubbling around the edges around 10 minutes. It may brown faster if you keep an eye on it.
7) If you haven't already, if you haven't already added them to the dessert before baking, serve it hot.

# MELT-IN-MOUTH BUTTER COOKIES (EGYPTIAN GHORAYEBAH)

Cook Time: 25 minutes

Servings: 8-10 servings

## INGREDIENTS

- 1 cup/195 g ghee (highly clarified butter like this kind)
- ½ cup/ 63.77 g powdered sugar, sifted, and more for later
- scant ⅛ tsp/ 0.5 g baking powder
- 2 cups/ 240 g all-purpose flour, sifted
- Handful slivered almonds (optional)

## INSTRUCTIONS

1) Place ghee in a large mixing bowl. Using a hand-held electric mixer like this one, mix on low until ghee is whipped.
2) Add powdered sugar, then mix again using hand mixer. Start mixer on low and then increase speed as needed to medium until the ghee-sugar mixture is whipped (should look smooth and fluffy.)
3) Set the mixer aside. Add baking powder, then add 1 cup flour. Knead with your hand to work flour in, then add the remaining 1 cup flour. Knead again until flour is well incorporated into a super soft dough.
4) Cover and refrigerate for 20 minutes so that the dough will firm up a bit. Meanwhile, preheat oven to 350 degrees F (see tip #2). And prepare a baking sheet lined with parchment paper.
5) When ready, remove dough from fridge. Take small portions of dough (heaping ½ tablespoons) and form into small walnut-sized balls. Ever so lightly press the top (do not flatten). Arrange on prepared baking sheet, about 2 to 3 inches or so apart.
6) Lightly press a slivered almond on each or some of the cookies.
7) Bake in heated oven for 12 to 15 minutes or so (cookies should firm up and gain a bit of color on the bottom. But should remain pretty light in color on top.)
8) Remove from oven. Do NOT touch cookies until cooled (they will fall apart). Sprinkle powdered sugar on top. Enjoy!
9)

# MAJBOOS/ KABSA – MEAT AND VEGETABLES RICE

Prep Time: 10 minutes

Cook Time: 1 hour

Servings: 6 servings

## INGREDIENTS

- 2 and ½ cup of Basmati Rice
- 10 pieces of Chicken Leg, Thigh and Wings
- 1 cup of chopped onion
- 5 cloves of garlic
- Water for boiling the chicken
- 1 cup of water if the chicken stock is not enough to boil the rice (Optional)

**Spices and Herbs**

- 2 Black Lemon / Lime
- 6 Bay Leaf
- 6 cloves
- 5 to 6 Cardamom Pods
- ½ teaspoon of cumin
- ¼ teaspoon of cinnamon powder
- 1 teaspoon of curry
- ¾ teaspoon of coriander
- ½ teaspoon of turmeric
- Salt and Black Pepper for Taste

## INSTRUCTIONS

1) Put the heat on. Add water to the cooking pot after placing the chicken there. Let the chicken bubble.
2) While the chicken is bubbling, eliminate the overabundance fats from the chicken.
3) Add the spices, onion, and garlic to the boiling pot after the fats are removed. Allow it to bubble for 45 minutes or until the chicken is delicate.
4) Eliminate the onion, garlic, and other strong fixings. You now have the stock, which you can use later by separating them from the chicken stock. Add the long-grain or basmati rice to the stock. Add more water if the stock is not sufficient.
5) while the rice is being cooked. In a separate pan, add oil and fry the chicken until it has a nice brown, crispy texture. Place the chicken on top of the rice that has already been cooked. Before serving, well combine them with the rice. Decorated with parsley

# GURSAN – MEAT AND VEGETABLE STEW

Prep Time: 10 minutes

Cook Time: 45 minutes

Servings: 6 servings

## INGREDIENTS

- 500 g boned lamb meat
- 3 carrots
- 4 ground tomatoes
- 1 eggplant
- 1 tbsp garlic paste
- 2 dried lemons
- 3 zucchini
- 1 small potato
- 200 g pumpkin
- 100 g green beans
- 2 tbsp tomato paste
- 2 chopped onions
- 1 red chili
- 1 tbsp Saudi spices
- 1 tbsp coriander powder
- 1 tbsp cumin powder
- ½ tsp turmeric
- 1 tbsp salt
- 1 tbsp honey
- Dried Gursan bread

## INSTRUCTIONS

1) Cut the pumpkin, carrots, eggplant, zucchini, potato, and others into large chunks.
2) Add 6 tbsp of oil to a pot and heat on medium-high.
3) Cook the garlic and onions until they are golden brown.
4) Cook the meat, cumin, coriander, turmeric, tomato paste, and Saudi spices for five minutes.
5) Cook for ten minutes before adding ground tomatoes.
6) Add 2 liters of water and cook meat covered for 35 minutes.
7) Cook for five minutes before adding the carrots, green beans, dried lemon, and red chili.
8) Cook the pumpkin, potato, eggplant, and zucchini for ten minutes.

9) Layer small pieces of Gursan bread and a little sauce with vegetables in a deep serving bowl. Layer more Gursan bread on top, then drizzle some sauce with vegetables over it. Continue to rehash this cycle until the dish is full.
10) Place the meat on top, then add fried onions and coriander that has just been chopped.

## JALAMAH – ARABIAN LAMB STEW

Prep Time: 15 minutes

Cook Time: 55 minutes

Servings: 4-6 servings

## INGREDIENTS

- Meat cut into small pieces and meat with bone also small pieces and quantity as you like
- fat also cut into small pieces(Little bit more then small).
- 2 onion chopped
- salt
- black pepper
- green pepper
- 5 cardamon pods
- Cinnamon powder
- Coriander powder

## INSTRUCTIONS

1) preparation without washing the meat and fat (shaham) separately.
2) Add the meat, salt, onion, and spices to a large saucepan and cook over high heat, removing any excess fat. Perform shifting each two minutes.
3) control the heat by moving the fat until it turns gold.
4) Then, carefully add the meat and shift every three-quarters minute until it turns brown.
5) then get a small, fat saucepan.
6) Then, add the spices (black pepper, cardamom, cinnamon, and coriander powder) and cook until done. Store at room temperature. One of the characteristics of meat-eaters is that it keeps meat for a long time—up to a year.

# DAJAJ MASHWI – ARABIAN GRILLED CHICKEN

Prep Time: 20 minutes

Cook Time: 30 minutes

Servings: 2 serving

## INGREDIENTS

- 300 grams Chicken Wings , boneless
- 2 tablespoon Extra Virgin Olive Oil , (Extra virgin)
- 1 tablespoon Paprika powder
- 1 tablespoon Black pepper powder
- 1 tablespoon Dried oregano
- 1 tablespoon Mint Leaves (Pudina) , (dried)
- Salt , to taste
- 1 teaspoon Garlic , crushed

## INSTRUCTIONS

1) To make Dajaj Mechwi Recipe, thoroughly clean the chicken. Wipe off on a kitchen towel.
2) Beat the chicken thoroughly in a zip-lock bag.
3) Mix all the spices now. Rub the chicken with olive oil.
4) Cover the chicken with the spice mixture. To marinate, place it in the refrigerator for 30 minutes.
5) If you're using a charcoal grill, heat it up. Now, place the pieces of marinated chicken on the grill.
6) Barbecue until chicken is cooked, continue to flip at normal spans.
7) Serve the grilled Dajaj Mechwi Recipe right away with crusty bread, ratatouille, grilled cottage cheese steak, and salad after it has been removed from the pan.

# RUZ AL BUKHARI – FRAGRANT RICE AND ROASTED CHICKEN

Prep Time: 30 minutes

Cook Time: 30 minutes

Servings: 6 servings

## INGREDIENTS

### Chicken

- 1000 g chicken breast
- 2 small garlic cloves
- 1 tsp salt
- 1 tsp black pepper
- 6 tbsp olive oil
- ½ tsp kabsa spice mix see details further down

### Rice

- 600 g basmati rice 3 cups
- 4 tbsp butter preferably ghee/clarified butter
- 1400 ml chicken broth 6 cups
- 2 pinches turmeric
- 2 small carrots
- 4 tbsp raisins
- salt

### Daqous (Spiced Tomato Sauce)

- 950 ml finely crushed tomatoes / tomato puree 4 cups
- 2 tbsp tomato paste
- salt
- black pepper
- 2 tsp olive oil
- 2 pinches cumin
- 2 tsp tahini roasted sesame paste
- 8 garlic cloves
- ½ tsp baharat spice mix see details further down

### Baharat spice mix (mix all ingredients together and use only ½ tsp)

- 1 tbsp black pepper
- ½ tbsp ground coriander
- ½ tbsp ground cinnamon

- ½ tbsp ground cloves
- ½ tbsp ground cumin
- ½ tsp ground cardamom
- ½ tsp ground nutmeg
- 1 tbsp paprika powder

**Kabsa spice mix (mix all ingredients together and use only ½ tsp)**

- ½ tsp saffron
- ¼ tsp ground cardamom
- ½ tsp ground cinnamon
- ½ tsp ground allspice
- ¼ tsp black pepper
- ½ tsp ground dried lime
- ¼ tsp ground fennel seeds optional
- ¼ tsp ground coriander optional

## INSTRUCTIONS

1) Season chicken breasts with olive oil, salt and pepper and Kabsa spice mix.
2) Cook the chicken on the grill or in the oven, turning occasionally until cooked through.
3) Rinse the rice well and soak in cold water for 20 minutes. Drain.
4) In a deep pan melt butter, add grated carrots and raisins, sauté.
5) Add the remaining ingredients, bring to boil, reduce heat and simmer covered on low heat for 15-20 minutes until done.
6) Mix all the ingredients in a medium pot.
7) Simmer over low heat, while stirring, until well combined.
8) Add more liquid if needed (water or chicken broth).
9) Serve chicken with rice, daqqūs and a green salad.

# THARID/ THAREED – MEAT AND VEGETABLE STEW OVER CRISPY BREAD

Prep Time: 35 minutes

Cook Time: 1.5 hours

Servings: 4-6 servings

## INGREDIENTS

- 4 ½ pounds/2 kilograms boneless lamb shoulder or leg, or neck fillets
- 2 ounces/60 grams beef caul fat (ask your butcher for this), chopped
- 2 ½ quarts water
- 2 large heirloom or vine-ripe tomatoes
- 4 inches/10 cm fresh ginger, peeled and cut into chunks
- 2 whole garlic cloves, peeled
- 1 medium yellow onion, quartered
- 2 tablespoons tomato paste
- 4 black dried limes, pierced in a few places
- 2 bay leaves
- 2 chiles de árbol
- 2 tablespoons B'zar (Arabian Spice Mixture; see recipe below)
- 1 tablespoon ground cumin
- 1 teaspoon freshly ground black pepper
- ¼ teaspoon ground cardamom
- ¼ teaspoon whole cloves
- 18 petite finger-size carrots, trimmed and peeled
- 18 baby Yukon gold potatoes
- 18 baby zucchini
- 2 to 3 handkerchief breads; see note above, toasted until crisp but not browned
- ¼ cup whole black peppercorns
- ¼ cup whole cumin seeds
- ¼ cup whole coriander seeds
- 1 tablespoon whole cloves
- 1 tablespoon broken Ceylon cinnamon sticks
- 1 tablespoon whole green cardamom pods
- 1 tablespoon crumbled chiles de arbol
- 1 whole nutmeg, broken into small pieces
- 1 tablespoon ground ginger
- 1 tablespoon ground turmeric

## INSTRUCTIONS

1) Place the meat, caul fat and water in a large pot and bring to a boil over medium heat. Drain off the broth and pour the same amount of clean water over the meat. This will ensure you have a clean-tasting broth.
2) Combine the tomatoes, fresh ginger, garlic and onion in a food processor and process until completely puréed. Add the tomato purée to the lamb along with the tomato paste, dried limes, bay leaves, chiles and spices and bring to a boil. Reduce the heat to maintain a gentle simmer and cook, uncovered, until the lamb is tender, about 1 hour.
3) Add the carrots and potatoes and cook for 10 minutes. Add the zucchini and cook for 10 more minutes.
4) 1 sheet of toasted handkerchief bread in a shallow serving dish. Pour enough lamb broth over the bread to let it become soft but not soupy. Spread another layer of broken bread and add more broth. Make another layer, softening the bread with broth until you have a fairly thick layer of moistened bread, about 2 inches/5 cm deep.
5) Arrange the meat and vegetables over the bread and serve immediately.

## JAREESH– CRUSHED WHEAT WITH MEAT

Prep Time: 45 minutes

Cook Time: 4 hours

Servings: 6-8 servings

## INGREDIENTS

- 2 lb lamb neck or shoulder with bone
- 6 cups pearl wheat
- ¾ cup ghee clarified butter
- Water
- Salt
- Pepper

**For the seasoning**

**Option 1**

- ½ teaspoon ground cinnamon
- 2 teaspoons ground and roasted cumin

**Option 2**

- 4 cloves garlic chopped
- 6 pods cardamom

**Option 3**

- ½ teaspoon cinnamon
- 3 tablespoons caster sugar

## INSTRUCTIONS

1. The wheat should be soaked for eight hours in a lot of cold water.
2. In a huge pot, place the pre-drenched and depleted wheat, add 1 quart (1 liter) of water, cover and bubble until the wheat starts to expand and mellow somewhat, around 30 minutes.
3. Soak the lamb in a large amount of lightly salted water while the wheat is being cooked.
4. Rinse the meat and drain it when the wheat is soft.
5. Place the wheat and meat in a heavy bottom or large cast-iron pot. Add salt and pepper to taste.
6. Water should be covered by about 2 inches (5 cm) above the meat and wheat. Cover.
7. After coming to a boil over high heat, reduce the heat and cook for four hours on very low heat, stirring every so often to get rid of any foam or fat from the surface.
8. Remove the pot from the heat and allow the wheat to cool slightly before removing the bones once it is very soft, has lost its shape, and has absorbed most of the water.
9. Add about 250 milliliters (250 milliliters) of boiling water if all the water has been absorbed. If the wheat is cooked but there is too much water, drain the excess water.
10. If there are any larger pieces of lamb, shred them. Because almost all of the meat will have melted in the wheat, there shouldn't be any.
11. Utilizing a medhrab (a uniquely planned wooden blender) or an enormous wooden spoon, beat the wheat and meat enthusiastically until you get the consistency of homogeneous and marginally versatile porridge.
12. This can be done by hand, but you can also use a hand blender or a food processor to blend it.
13. Keep warm while adjusting the seasoning.
14. Add the seasonings of your choice to the ghee in a large pot and season to taste with salt and pepper.
15. Mix thoroughly as you warm the ghee over low heat.
16. Add the seasoned ghee to a large earthenware dish and cover the wheat porridge.
17. Serve right away.

# SALEEG – ROASTED MEAT & CREAMY RICE

Prep Time: 30 minutes

Cook Time: 70 Minutes

Servings: 4-6 Servings

## INGREDIENTS

### For the Chicken Stock

- 1 kg chicken whole legs 4 to 5 whole legs
- 8 cups water
- 3 green cardamom
- 3 cloves
- 1 inch cinnamon stick
- ½ teaspoon black peppercorns
- 1 small piece galangal root (optional)
- 1 small piece black stone flower black stone flower (optional)
- 1 medium onion peeled and quartered
- salt to taste

### For the Rice

- 6 cups chicken stock
- 2 cups hot water
- 2 mastic beads crushed (optional)
- 2 cups short-grain rice rinsed and soaked (mix of Egyptian or Calrose rice and American rice or jeerakasala rice)
- 1 cup full-fat milk
- 2 tablespoons ghee or butter

To roast the boiled Chicken

- 2 tablespoons ghee or butter
- 1 tablespoon Arab spice mix (bezar or baharat etc.)

## INSTRUCTIONS

1. Place chicken pieces in a stockpot along with the whole spices, onions and enough water.
2. 1 kg chicken whole legs,8 cups water,3 green cardamom,3 cloves,1 inch cinnamon stick,½ teaspoon black peppercorns,1 small piece galangal root,1 medium onion,6 cups chicken stock,1 small piece black stone flower
3. Bring the water to a full boil and then carefully skim the froth that appears on the top and discard it until the stock is clear.
4. 8 cups water
5. Reduce the flame to medium and allow to cook for 30 minutes or until the chicken is done.
6. Remove the chicken pieces with the help of a tong and keep them aside in a skillet.
7. Strain the stock to get rid of the whole spices and onion. You can either strain it into another pot in which you intend to make the Saleeg or into a bowl and transfer it back into the same pot.
8. Prepare the rice
9. In the same pot, add the chicken stock, crushed mastic tear, rice, hot water and salt to taste.
10. 6 cups chicken stock,2 cups hot water,2 mastic beads,2 cups short-grain rice
11. Bring this to a full boil, reduce heat to low and cover the pot. Cook for 20 minutes stirring every now and then.
12. Open and add the milk, and butter and give it a good stir.
13. 1 cup full-fat milk,2 tablespoons ghee or butter,salt to taste
14. Check and add salt and cook on low stirring every now and then.
15. salt to taste
16. Cook until the rice is creamy and thick not dry and sticky! If you feel it is dry, add some more hot milk and stir again. You may add some cream cheese for more creaminess.
17. Roast the chicken
18. Roast the chicken on the stovetop or in a preheated oven. You may mix any Arabic seasoning with butter to rub on the boiled chicken and roast until browned.
19. 1 tablespoon Arab spice mix,2 tablespoons ghee or butter
20. Serve Saleeg
21. On a wide plate pour the prepared Saleeg, smooth the top and place the roasted chicken in the middle. Serve with Salata Hara and some salad.

# MANDI – CHICKEN RICE

Prep Time: 15 minutes

Cook Time: 1 hour 15 minutes

Servings: 6-8 servings

## INGREDIENTS

### For the Spice Blend

- 2 teaspoons whole coriander seeds
- 1 teaspoon whole cloves
- 6 green cardamom pods
- 1.5 teaspoons cumin seeds
- 1 cinnamon stick
- 1 teaspoon whole black peppercorns
- ½ teaspoon turmeric (ground powder)

### For the Chicken

- 4 full chicken legs, skin on, bone in
- 2 tablespoons olive oil
- 1.5 teaspoons kosher salt use 1 tsp if regular salt

### For the Rice

- 3 cups basmati rice
- 3 bay leaves
- 2 teaspoons spice mix (from the spice blend)
- 1.5 teaspoon turmeric
- ½ teaspoon saffron strands plus 2 tablespoons hot water (optional)
- 3 dried limes optional
- 1 teaspoon salt
- 4.5 cups water and broth see instructions

### For the Garnish

- 4 small onions
- 1 cup vegetable oil for frying
- ¼ cup slivered almonds
- ¼ cup raisins
- 1 tablespoon olive oil

# INSTRUCTIONS

### For the Spice Blend:

1) Start by placing all of the spices for the blend except for the turmeric in a small skillet and toast on medium heat for 1-2 minutes, moving them around constantly. Be careful as they burn fast! Remove them as soon as they start to become really fragrant.

2) Once toasted, remove and place in a spice or coffee grinder and grind until a fine powder forms
3) Remove 2 teaspoons from the spice mix and set aside for the rice. Add the turmeric to the remainder of the spice mix and set aside to be used for the chicken
4) To Marinate The Chicken:
5) To the spice blend, add the ½ teaspoon turmeric and the 1.5 teaspoons kosher salt listed under the chicken
6) Add 1 tablespoon of the olive oil to the spice mix and create a paste. Lather the paste onto the chicken legs and massage it in really well.
7) Place the marinated chicken in an airtight container and marinate overnight in the fridge for optimal results. If you can't do this, you can marinate for 30 mins to 1 hour to save time.
8) To Fry the Onions:
9) Thinly slice all of the onions evenly. I do this by hand but if you want to be precise you can always use a mandolin (even size helps them fry evenly)
10) Add the one cup of vegetable oil to the pot (the same pot you will cook rice in) and heat on medium heat
11) Add the onions in and fry them, stirring them every 3-4 minutes. This process will take 10-15 minutes, so be patient! But also be careful, towards the end, they will burn fast so keep a watchful eye and remove them quickly.
12) Remove the onions when they look golden brown, leaving approximately 3 tablespoons of onions in the pot for the rice. Spread on a paper towel lined plate to absorb the oil. As they cool they will crisp up (see notes). Set aside until ready to garnish.

### To Cook the Chicken:

13) The chicken will cook by steaming. Start this process after marinating the chicken. To the pot that you fried the onions in (and with the remaining onions and oil inside), add the spice mix that was set aside for the rice
14) Carefully pierce the dry limes a couple of times using a sharp knife (be careful because they are round!) and add them to the pot along with the bay leaves
15) Cook the spices in the oil on medium heat for a few minutes. Add 2 cups of water.
16) Place a steaming rack in the pot (if you don't have a steaming rack, use a small wire rack similar to an instant pot insert). Place the marinated chicken on the steaming rack.
17) Close the pot lid and steam the chicken for 50 minutes on medium heat. Check it every 10 minutes to ensure there is enough water and top it up if not.

18) Remove the chicken (reserve the broth) when cooked through and place on an oven baking tray (preferably on an over wire rack placed on top of a tray, but you can use a tray too).
19) Brush the top with the remaining olive oil and bake for 20 mins at 400F. Broil the top for 5 minutes until golden brown. Remove and keep warm.

**To Make the Rice:**

20) Wash the rice really well multiple times until the water runs clear, then soak for 10 minutes
21) In a mortar and pestle, grind the saffron to a fine powder then add 2 tablespoons of hot water (boiled water that has cooled slightly) and bloom for 5 minutes
22) Strain the broth that was used to steam the chicken. Using a measuring cup, measure out how much broth you have and add to it some water (if required) to get exactly 4.5 cups of liquid
23) Pour the liquid back into the same pot. Add to it the turmeric listed under rice, the salt and the bloomed saffron. Taste and ensure it is visibly salty (like sea water). Allow it to come to a boil.
24) Add the rice to the broth and stir a few times to combine. Allow it to come to a boil uncovered for a few minutes on medium heat.
25) Once bubbling, place a paper towel on top of the pot and then close the lid. Lower the heat to medium low and allow it to cook for 20 minutes, undisturbed.
26) After 20 minutes, turn the heat off and fluff with a fork. Close the lid and allow it to stand for 10 minutes.

**For the Garnish:**

27) The first layer of garnish will be the fried onions
28) To prepare the almonds, cook them on medium heat with the olive oil until golden. Stir continuously. Remove and set aside
29) Add the raisins in and toast for 2 minutes. Combine with the almonds.
30) To Assemble:
31) In a large platter, layer the yellow rice
32) Add the fried onions, almonds and raisins
33) Add the chicken, then add more onions, raisins and almonds. Garnish with chopped parsley if desired
34) Serve with a side of salad, yogurt, or Yemeni Zhoug and enjoy!

# MASOUB ~ SAUDI BANANA BREAD MASH

Prep Time: 5 minutes

Cook Time: 10 minutes

Servings: 2 servings

## INGREDIENTS

- 1 tsp ghee
- 2 ripe bananas mashed
- 1 tbsp sugar
- 4 wholemeal bread powdered
- A pinch cinnamon powder
- For topping:
- 3 tbsp cream
- 1 tbsp honey
- 5-6 almonds sliced

## INSTRUCTIONS

1. Heat ghee in a saucepan.
2. Add the mashed bananas, sprinkle the sugar and briefly saute it.
3. Add in the bread along with cinnamon powder and mix it well till nicely combined.
4. Cook for a couple of minutes and switch off. Transfer to a serving dish and flatten the top.
5. Spread the cream on the top, drizzle honey and sprinkle the almonds.
6. Enjoy warm!

# SOBIA DRINK

Prep Time: 15 minutes

Servings: 4-6 servings

## INGREDIENTS

- 3 pieces of white bread.
- 3 pieces of brown bread.
- 3 tablespoons of oats.
- 4 dried dates
- A teaspoon of ground cinnamon.
- A teaspoon of ground cardamom.
- A teaspoon of rose water.
- 4 cups of water.
- sugar as desired.
- Red food color or any color you prefer

## INSTRUCTIONS

1. Cut the bread into small pieces and put them on a large plate.
2. Add oats and dates, put half the amount of cinnamon and cardamom, then add water.
3. Leave the ingredients to soak for at least a day in the refrigerator, stirring from time to time.
4. Strain the ingredients using a piece of cheesecloth, and add the sugar along with the rest of the cinnamon, cardamom and food coloring.
5. The ingredients are mixed in an electric mixer, and put in the refrigerator until cold.
6. Pour into glasses, store the drink in the refrigerator, and serve cold during breakfast.

## JALLAB

Prep Time: 5 minutes

Servings: 1 serving

## INGREDIENTS

- 3 Tbsp store-bought Jallab syrup
- 1 Tbsp golden raisins
- 1 Tbsp pine nuts
- Crushed ice

## INSTRUCTIONS

1. Put the Jallab syrup in a tall glass, top with cold water and stir
2. Add as much crushed ice as you like
3. Top the drink with the raisins and pine nuts

## JORDANIAN MANSAF

Prep Time: 30 minutes

Cook Time: 120 minutes

Servings: 6-8 servings

## INGREDIENTS

- 2 lbs lean lamb (can be substituted with beef)
- 1/2 cup butter
- Salt
- Pepper
- 1 medium onion. Finely chopped.
- 2 cups plain Greek yogurt
- 1 egg white
- 1/2 tsp. coriander
- 1 1/2 tsp. cumin
- 1/2 tsp. paprika
- 1/4 tsp. cardamom
- 1/2 cup whole blanched almonds
- 1/2 cup pine nuts
- 4-6 loaves pita bread or naan
- 3 cups uncooked rice

- parsley or chives for garnish

## INSTRUCTIONS

1. Place meat cubes in a container with a lid after being rinsed.
2. Place the meat in the refrigerator for four to eight hours and cover it with water.
3. Heat a skillet to medium-high heat when you are ready to cook. Liquefy 1/4 margarine in a skillet.
4. Using a paper towel, drain and pat dry meat cubes.
5. Cook the meat on all sides in the melted butter until it is browned.
6. Salt and pepper the meat to taste.
7. To just cover the meat, add enough water. Cook for one hour on low heat.
8. Cover and simmer for 30 minutes before adding the onion.
9. Place the yogurt in a large sauce pan over medium heat while the meat and onion simmer. The yogurt should be whisked until it resembles liquid. Add 1/2 teaspoon and the egg white with a whisk. of course.
10. The yogurt mixture should be boiling. Using a wooden spoon, stir consistently in one direction. After it has reached a boil, turn down the heat to low and let the yogurt mixture simmer, covered, for ten minutes.
11. The yogurt mixture should be added to the meat. Season to taste.
12. Adjust the seasoning as necessary during the 15 minutes of simmering on low.
13. In a little skillet liquefy 2 tbsp. from butter Cook for five minutes after adding the almonds. Add the pine nuts and cook for an additional three minutes. Remove from heat and set aside when finished.
14. Spread open the pita or naan and orchestrate on a huge serving plate. ( I like to have them pieces fallen to pieces for simple scooping). 2 tbsp is used to brush the bread. from butter
15. Organize the rice over the bread passing on a well at the middle to put the meat.
16. Place the meat in the well and cover it with the butter-nut mixture.
17. Use chives or parsley as a garnish.

# LABNEH (STRAINED YOGURT)

Prep Time: 5 minutes

Resting Time: 12 hours

Servings: 8 servings

## INGREDIENTS

- 500 g (2 cups) yoghurt whole milk
- 1 tsp salt
- 3 tsp olive oil for garnish
- 1 pinch zaatar for garnish, optional

## INSTRUCTIONS

1. Mix yogurt and salt in a large bowl. Stir to combine.
2. Place a linen cloth on a fine mesh strainer. Add the yogurt mixture onto the cloth. Cover with the sides of the cloth.
3. Place the strainer on a large bowl. Strain for at least 12 hours.
4. Remove the strained yogurt from the cloth to a flat bowl or plate. Garnish with olive oil, za'atar and finely chopped parsley leaves.

# MANAQISH | JORDANIAN ZAATAR FLATBREAD ~ J FOR JORDAN

Prep Time: 10 minutes

Cook Time: 20 minutes

Servings: 2-3 servings

## INGREDIENTS

- 3 cups All Purpose Flour
- 2 tsp Active Dry Yeast / Instant Yeast - 1.33 tsp
- 1 cup Warm Water
- 1 tsp Sugar
- 1 tsp Salt

### For spreading

- 4 tbsp Zaatar Spice Blend
- 2 tbsp Olive Oil
- 1/2 tsp Lemon Juice

## INSTRUCTIONS

1. If you are using active dry yeast, proof it by combining it with sugar and warm water in a bowl. Cover it and stir it around. Trust that the yeast will froth and afterward use. Before kneading, instant yeast can be added directly to the flour.
2. Add the yeast mix or instant yeast to the flour, salt, and large bowl. To form a soft, pliable dough, thoroughly combine everything and gradually add water.
3. Cover it and let it sit for an hour or until it doubles in size.
4. Blend the zaatar with olive oil and lemon juice. Punch the dough down and flour it after it has doubled in size. Roll out equal-sized discs, sprinkle with the zaatar mix, and bake in a preheated oven for 8 to 10 minutes, or until the dough is cooked through. Serve the dip warm.

## KOUSA MAHSHI (STUFFED ZUCCHINI)

Prep Time: 35 minutes

Cook Time: 50 minutes

Servings: 2-3 servings

## INGREDIENTS

- 1 cup basmati rice
- 15 small zucchini (Mexican or Lebanese zucchini)
- 1 pound ground beef
- 1 (14.5 ounce) can diced tomatoes
- ½ medium yellow onion, finely chopped
- ¼ cup chopped parsley
- ¼ cup chopped mint
- 2 tablespoons olive oil
- 1 teaspoon cumin
- 1 teaspoon ground black pepper
- 3 teaspoons salt, divided
- ½ teaspoon paprika
- ½ teaspoon ground coriander
- ½ teaspoon ground cinnamon
- 1 (14.5 ounce) can tomato sauce
- water

## INSTRUCTIONS

1. Add the rice to a bowl and top it off with sufficient water to cover the rice. Allow the rice to drench while you set up the zucchini.
2. Remove the end from the zucchini's smaller side. Using an apple corer or a zucchini corer, carefully core the zucchini, leaving about 18 inches around all sides. Cut through the zucchini with care.
3. Ground beef, diced tomatoes, parsley, mint, olive oil, cumin, black pepper, 1 teaspoon of salt, paprika, coriander, and cinnamon are all added to the rice after it has been drained. Use a spoon or your hands to mix the ingredients until they are well-combined.
4. Delicately stuff every zucchini with a couple of tablespoons of the rice meat combination. Fill the zucchini to the brim with the mixture, but leave a 12-inch space at the top.
5. In a large pot, stack the zucchini on top of each other. Empty the pureed tomatoes into the pot, alongside the excess 2 teaspoons of salt. Fill the zucchini with sufficient water to cover them all.
6. To keep the zucchini in place, place a small plate on top of them.
7. Place the pot on the stove and cover it with a lid. Over medium-high heat, bring the sauce to a low simmer. Reduce the heat, cover, and simmer for 50 to 1 hour, or until the rice is tender and the beef is cooked.
8. If desired, top with a dollop of minted yogurt.

# WARAK ENAB- STUFFED GRAPE LEAVES

Prep Time: 60 minutes

Cook Time: 120 minutes

Servings: 6 servings

## INGREDIENTS

- For the rice stuffing:
- 1.5 cups Egyptian rice (short grain rice)
- 1-2 small tomato, very finely diced
- 1-2 small onion, very finely diced,
- 1/4 cup fresh parsley, minced
- 2 cloves garlic, crushed
- 1.5 teaspoon seven spices or all spice
- 1/4 teaspoon cinnamon powder
- 2 teaspoon salt
- 1/2 teaspoon black pepper
- 2 tablespoon olive oil
- 200 g ground lamb
- To assemble:
- 1 jar vine leaves (450 g or 1 lb)
- 6-8 zucchini (koosa), cored
- 2-3 eggplants, cored
- 2 tomatoes sliced
- 2 potatoes sliced
- 1 lb lamb chops or lamb neck pieces 1/2 kg
- salt and pepper to taste
- olive oil
- 3 lemons, juiced
- 2-3 tablespoon tomato paste
- boiling water to cover the the stuffed grape leaves (or vegetable or chicken broth)

## INSTRUCTIONS

1. Soak the Egyptian rice for 20 minutes or so, then rinse with cold water until water runs clear.
2. Place rice in a large bowl and add the tomato, onion, parsley, garlic, spices, and olive oil and stir well to combine. Add the raw minced lamb, and stir to evenly incorporate into the rice mixture. It might be easier to use your hands to work the meat into the rice.
3. Place the vine leaves in a bowl of hot water for 3 minutes. This helps them lose a little of the brininess. Drain, and gently separate vine leaves.

4. Stuff the cored zucchini and eggplant until 3/4 filled with rice. Use your finger to pack them firmly. Set aside.
5. Stuff the vine leaves by placing an individual leaf with the tip pointing upwards, placing a heaped teaspoon of the rice stuffing in the center of the vine leave, folding sides towards the center, then rolling from the bottom upwards, tucking in the sides of the vine leaves as you go. It's like you're making a sandwich wrap. Keep going until you've finished all the stuffing.
6. Place a layer of tomatoes at the bottom of a large, heavy bottomed saucepan. Layer your potato slices on top of the tomato. This will keep the vine leaves touching the bottom of the pan from burning, plus they are delicious.
7. Season the lamb chops or lamb neck with salt and pepper, and place on top of the potato slices.
8. Place the stuffed zucchini and eggplant in a ring around the circumference of the pot, then gently place the stuffed vine leaves in an even layer filling the rest of the pot, like pictured above.
9. Drizzle olive oil over the top of the filled pot. Add boiling water to the pot, pouring at the edge of the pot until the water just comes to the top layer of the vine leaves- the top layer shouldn't be submerged. Sprinkle with salt to season. Place a plate on top of the vine leaves to hold them down so the vine leaves don't float around while cooking. Cover the pot with a tightly fitting lid.
10. Bring the pot to a boil, then reduce heat to medium low and let the fluid in the pot come to a simmer. Simmer for anywhere between 1.5-2.5 hours, or until vine leaves and stuffed vegetables are cooked through and the rice inside is cooked through. Start checking at the 1 hour mark. 15 minutes before you take the pot off the heat, add the lemon juice.
11. Once the meal is ready, flip the vine leaves onto a large serving plate carefully, make sure it has higher edges because a lot of broth will come out. Serve immediately and enjoy with some yogurt on the side. These are also very tasty at room temperature or cold!

# KIBBEH

Prep Time: 2 hours 15 minutes

Servings: 25-30 pieces

## INGREDIENTS

- 2 ½ cups fine bulgur wheat
- Water
- 1 large onion, quartered
- 1 ½ lb lean ground beef (or lamb)
- 2 tsp ground allspice
- 1 tsp ground coriander
- ½ tsp ground cinnamon
- 1 tsp black pepper
- Pinch salt
- Oil for frying
- For the Meat Filling
- Olive oil
- 1 medium yellow onion, finely chopped or grated
- 1 lb ground lamb or beef (I used beef here), cold
- ⅓ cup toasted pine nuts
- 1 tsp ground allspice
- ½ tsp ground cinnamon
- Pinch salt and pepper

## INSTRUCTIONS

1. Cover a fine mesh strainer with a light cloth (a cheesecloth, if you have one). Add the bulgur wheat in, then place the strainer into a bowl filled with water. Let the fine bulgur wheat soak in the water for 15 minutes, then pull the cloth, holding the bulgur, and squeeze all the water out. You may do this a couple of times until you are sure the bulgur is rid of water. Set aside for now.
2. Now make the kibbeh (the actual dough that you will later use to form the kibbeh shells). Put the onion, ground beef, spices and pinch of salt into the bowl of a large food processor. Process until the meat is very finely ground almost into a paste. Transfer the meat mixture into a large bowl and add the bulgur wheat. Use damp hands to combine the bulgur with the meat mixture to make a dough. Cover and refrigerate until later.
3. Now make the filling. Heat about 1 tablespoon olive oil in a skillet or frying pan. Saute the onion until just golden, then add the ground beef. Cook over medium heat, stirring occasionally until the meat is fully browned. Add the toasted pine nuts, the spices, and the salt and pepper. Stir to combine. Remove from the heat and set aside to cool.
4. Remove the kibbeh dough from the fridge.

5. To stuff the kibbeh, you need to have damp hands. Place a small bowl of water next to you. Prepare a baking sheet and line it with parchment paper.
6. With both the bowl of kibbeh dough and the filling near, you can begin stuffing the kibbeh. Dampen your hands with some water, take a handful of the kibbeh dough (about 2 tablespoon or so) and form into somewhat of an oval-shaped disc in the palm of one hand. Use your finger to make a well in the middle of the disc, and gradually hallow the disc out to make a larger well or hole for the filling. Using a spoon, add about 1 tablespoon of the filling. Seal the dough on top and, using both hands, carefully shape it into an oval (football-type shape). Place the stuffed kibbeh on the baking sheet lined with parchment paper. Repeat the stuffing steps until you run out, be sure to have damp hands throughout.
7. Chill the stuffed kibbeh for 1 hour.
8. Heat the oil in a deep frying pan to 350 degrees F (you'll want the oil hot enough that you can see some gentle bubbling, but not too hot where it will burn the kibbeh shells). Deep-fry the kibbeh in the hot oil, in batches being carefully not to crowd them, until the kibbeh shells are brown (about 5 minutes or so). With a slotted spoon or tongs, carefully remove the kibbeh and place them on a pan lined with paper towel to drain. Repeat until you have fried all the stuffed kibbeh.
9. Serve hot or at room temperature with tahini sauce, tzatziki sauce or plain Greek yogurt. Enjoy!

# MUSAKHAN (PALESTINIAN ROAST CHICKEN WITH SUMAC AND FLAT BREAD)

Prep Time: 60 minutes

Cook Time: 1 hour 20 minutes

Resting Time : 5 hours

Servings: 4-6 servings

## INGREDIENTS

### For the chicken and the marinade

- 1 free-range chicken (of about 2 lb / 1 kg), cut into pieces
- 4 cloves garlic
- 2 teaspoons allspice
- 1 teaspoon ground cumin
- 1 teaspoon ground cardamom
- 1 teaspoon ground cinnamon
- 5 tablespoons lemon juice , freshly squeezed

- 1 teaspoon ground coriander
- 2 teaspoons salt
- 1 tablespoon sumac
- 4 tablespoons olive oil

**For the sumac onions**

- 5 onions, cut into strips
- 3 tablespoons sumac
- ½ cup olive oil
- 3 tablespoons pine nuts, roasted
- 1 teaspoon salt
- 4 taboon flatbreads
- 1 small bunch cilantro, chopped

**Equipment**

- Mortar and pestle
- Baking dish

## INSTRUCTIONS

1) Peel the garlic and crush it finely in a mortar with a pestle.
2) Add all the spices, lemon juice and olive oil.
3) Place the chicken in a large bowl, rub it with the marinade, cover with plastic wrap and marinate for 5 hours in the refrigerator.
4) Take the chicken out of the refrigerator and place it at room temperature for 1 hour.
5) Preheat the oven to 350 F (180°C).
6) Place the chicken and the marinade in a deep baking dish and put it in the oven.
7) Cook for 1 hour.
8) Heat the olive oil in a pan over high heat and fry the onions for about 5 minutes, stirring regularly.
9) Place the pan on a medium heat and add the sumac and salt and mix well.
10) Let the onions caramelize for 10 to 15 minutes over medium heat, stirring regularly.
11) Remove the cooked chicken from the oven.
12) Remove the chicken from the baking dish.
13) Place the taboon in the baking dish and let it soak up the sauce.
14) Then place each taboon on a plate or large platter.
15) Spread caramelized sumac onions on top, place chicken on top and garnish with toasted pine nuts and chopped cilantro.

# JORDANIAN MANSAF

Prep Time: 2 hours 45 minutes

Servings: 8 servings

## INGREDIENTS

- 2 lbs lean lamb (1-1/2 inch cubes, beef can be substituted)
- 1/2 cup clarified butter (use samna or ghee if available, or make your clarified butter, see clarified butter note)
- salt
- pepper
- 1 medium onion, finely chopped
- 4 cups plain Greek yogurt
- 1 egg white
- 1 teaspoon pepper
- 1/2 teaspoon coriander (see spices note below)
- 1/2 teaspoons cumin
- 1/2 teaspoon paprika
- 1/4 teaspoon cardamom
- 1/2 cup whole blanched almond
- 1/2 cup pine nuts
- 4-6 loaves pita bread (khubz, Arabic pita-type bread is used in Jordan)
- 3 cups rice, raw measure, cooked (Jasmine med grain or Basmati is good)
- parsley or chives, chopped for garnish

## INSTRUCTIONS

1) Wash meat cubes and place in tray with lid. Cover meat with water, cover tray and place in refrigerator for 4-8 hours.
2) Melt 1/4 cup of the clarified butter in heavy skillet over medium-high heat. Drain and pat dry meat cubes. Place in skillet and cook for 20 minutes until browned on all sides. Season meat with salt and pepper, to taste, and add enough water to cover meat. Reduce heat, cover and cook for 1 hour. Add onion and simmer uncovered for 30 minutes.
3) While meat and onion are cooking, place yogurt in a large saucepan and whisk over medium heat until liquid. Whisk in egg white and ½ teaspoon of salt. Slowly bring yogurt mixture to boil stirring constantly with a wooden spoon in one direction only to reach desired consistency. Reduce heat to low and allow yogurt to softly simmer uncovered for 10 minutes.

4) Stir yogurt into meat and add seasonings as desired. Simmer gently for 15 minutes. Taste and adjust seasonings, as needed.
5) In a small skillet, melt 2 tablespoons of the remaining 4 tablespoons of clarified butter. Add almonds and cook for 5 minutes. Stir in pine nuts and cook for 3 minutes. Remove from heat and set aside.
6) Split the khubz loaves open and arrange, overlapping on a large serving tray. Melt the last remaining 2 tablespoons of butter and brush over the khubz to soften. Arrange rice over the khubz leaving a well in the center of the rice. Spoon the meat into the rice well and then spoon the butter and nuts over the meat. Sprinkle parsley or chives over top.

## SAYADIEH

Prep Time: 15 minutes

Cook Time: 30 minutes

Servings: 4-6 servings

# INGREDIENTS

- 1 lb Cod, cut into fillets or any white fish; like halibut
- 1 tbsp Cumin
- 1/2 tbsp Smoked Paprika
- Salt & pepper to taste
- 2 tbsp Filippo Berio Olive Oil for pan searing

**Rice Ingredients**

- 1.5 cups White Rice rinsed, and drained
- 1 tbsp Filippo Berio Olive oil
- 1 tbsp Cumin
- 1/4 tsp Turmeric
- 1 Bouillon Cube
- 3/4 Caramelized Cooked onions from below

**Caramelized Onions**

- 3 Yellow onions thinly sliced
- 2 tbsp Filippo Berio Olive Oil
- 1 tsp Cumin
- Salt & Pepper to taste

**Tahini Salad**

- 1 cup Parsley Finely chopped
- 1/2 cup Tomatoes Finely diced
- 3/4 cup Tahini
- 1 Large Lemon's juice add more for extra tanginess
- 1/2 cup Water to thin out salad, add more or less to your thickness preference
- 1 Garlic clove minced or crushed
- Salt to taste

## INSTRUCTIONS

1) First, mix together all the ingredients for the salad then set aside.
2) Secondly, prepare the onions by adding olive oil to a skillet then the onions and seasonings. Stir and cook on medium heat until the onions becomes caramelized and slightly crisp. 3/4 of the cooked onions will go to the rice and the rest as garnish.
3) To prepare the rice, add the rinsed rice to a pot with all the other ingredients then mix together. Add 3 cups of water or stock to this. Bring to a boil then a simmer and cook until fluffy and the water has evaporated.
4) For the fish, pat it dry then season on both sides with the above seasonings. Then, add the olive oil to a pan. You can use the same one the onions were cooked in. Have the stove on medium high heat then cook the fish for 4-5 minutes each side. Be very gentle when flipping the fish. The fish should be seared and cooked throughout.
5) To assemble, add the rice to the servings dish then top with the extra caramelized onions. Add the fish on top of that then add some toasted slivered almonds and parsley as garnish. Serve with the refreshing tahini salad. Enjoy!

# EGG SALAD

Cook Time: 5 minutes

## INGREDIENTS

- 12 eggs hard-boiled
- 1/3 cup kewpie mayo
- 1 tbsp mustard
- 2 tsp rice vinegar
- Three stalks of celery chopped
- One bunch of green onions chopped
- 1 tbsp relish
- One loaf of rustic bread
- One avocado sliced
- 1 tbsp hot sauce

## INSTRUCTIONS

1. Cook 12 eggs in an Instant Pot using the Egg Loaf or 5-5-5 methods.
2. Chop the eggs very finely. In a sizable mixing bowl, combine chopped eggs, celery, scallions, relish, mayo, Dijon, and vinegar. Add spicy Sauce to taste once everything is well combined.
3. Enjoy bread with egg salad and avocado slices on top!

# CHICKEN SHAWARMA RICE

Prep Time: 10 minutes

Cook Time: 35 minutes

Servings: 4-6 servings

## INGREDIENTS

- 2 tbsp extra-virgin olive oil
- 2 tbsp salted butter 1/4 stick
- One large red onion diced
- 2 lbs boneless deboned chicken thighs, cut into 1/4-inch-thick strips
- Three garlic cloves minced or pressed
- 3 cups garlic broth (e.g., Garlic Better than Bouillon) or chicken broth
- 1 tbsp paprika
- 1 tbsp curry powder
- 1 tbsp seasoned salt
- 1-2 tsp black pepper see Jeff's tips
- 1 1/2 tsp ground cumin
- 1 tsp turmeric

- 1 tsp ground cinnamon
- 1/2-1 tsp crushed red pepper flakes optional
- 1/2 tsp cayenne pepper optional
- 2 cups Basmati rice rinsed for 90 seconds and drained
- OPTIONAL WHITE GARLIC SAUCE
- 1 cup of plain whole milk yogurt, not Greek or flavored
- 1/4 cup mayonnaise
- 2 tbsp tahini optional
- Juice of 1/2 lemon
- Three garlic cloves minced or pressed
- 1 tbsp garlic powder
- 1/2 tsp lemon pepper seasoning
- 1/2 tsp cayenne pepper (optional for heat)
- 1/8–1/4 tsp garlic salt to taste
- OPTIONAL TOPPINGS
- tzatziki if not using the white garlic sauce and you want a shortcut
- Dill pickles diced

## INSTRUCTIONS

1. Butter and olive oil should be added to the Slow Cooker. Hit Sauté and change the setting to More or High. The onion should be added after the butter has melted and sautéed for 3 minutes, or until cooked and the color starts to dwindle.
2. Sauté the chicken and Garlic for about 3 minutes, until the chicken is pinkish-white in color.
3. Add the broth, cumin, turmeric, cinnamon, chopped red pepper flakes (if using), paprika, curry powder, spiced salt, black jalapeño, and cayenne pepper (if using). Stir often, scraping up any browned bits from the bottom of the saucepan as you go. Don't stir after adding the rice; smooth it on top.
4. Put the cover in Place, then turn the valve, so it is sealed. Press Manual or Cover And cook on High Press for 3 minutes, then press Cancel. Allow a 10-minute release free after the cooking is finished, then perform a fast getaway.
5. If used, combine the ingredients for the white garlic sauce in a sizable bowl, stir to incorporate, and set aside.
6. The rice should be combined, then placed on a serving plate and garnished with dill pickles and white garlic sauce (or tzatziki).

# FREEKEH

Prep Time: 10 minutes

Cook Time: 60 minutes

Servings : 6 servings

## INGREDIENTS

- 60 ml sunflower oil
- 40 g blanched almond halves
- 60 g pine nuts
- 30 g butter
- 500 g freekeh picked, rinsed several times and soaked in cold water for 30 minutes
- 1200 ml vegetable beef or chicken stock
- 1 ½ teaspoon salt or to taste
- ¼ teaspoon allspice
- ¼ black pepper or to taste
- 0.5 g to 1kg plain yoghurt to serve

## INSTRUCTIONS

1) Heat the oil in the large pot over medium heat and fry the pine nuts, stirring all the time, for about 2 minutes or until golden in colour. Remove with a slotted spoon onto a plate. Then fry the almonds, like the pine nuts, for 2 minutes and remove onto a plate. Reserve.
2) Add the butter to the oil in the large pot and sauté the drained freekeh for 2 minutes over moderate heat, stirring all the time. Season with the salt, the allspice and the black pepper and pour in the stock. Bring to a boil over high heat. Reduce to a simmer and cook, covered, for about 40 minutes or until the water is totally absorbed. Stir occasionally while cooking.
3) Spread freekeh over the serving platter and garnish with the pine nuts and the almonds. Serve as a main dish with some plain yoghurt or as a side dish with ablama or laban ummuh.

**THE END**

Printed in Great Britain
by Amazon